Joanna H. (Joanna Hooe) Mathews

Belle Powers' locket

Joanna H. (Joanna Hooe) Mathews

Belle Powers' locket

ISBN/EAN: 9783337041793

Printed in Europe, USA, Canada, Australia, Japan

Cover: Foto ©ninafisch / pixelio.de

More available books at **www.hansebooks.com**

LITTLE SUNBEAMS.

I.

BELLE POWERS' LOCKET.

By the same Author.

I.

THE BESSIE BOOKS.

Six vols. in a neat box. $7.50.

The volumes also sold separately; viz.: Bessie at the Seaside; City, Friends; Mountains; School; Travels, at $1.25 each.

"Really, it makes the heart younger, warmer, better, to bathe it afresh in such familiar, natural scenes, where benevolence of most practical and blessed utility is seen developing itself, from first to last, in such delightful symmetry and completeness as may, and we hope will, secure many imitators." — *Watchman and Reflector.*

II.

THE FLOWERETS.

A SERIES OF STORIES ON THE COMMANDMENTS.

Six vols. in a neat box. $3.60.

The vols. can also be had separately; viz.: 1. Violet's Idol; 2. Daisy's Work; 3. Rose's Temptation; 4. Lily's Lesson; 5. Hyacinthe and her Brothers; 6. Pinkie and the Rabbits, at 75 cents each.

"The child-world we are here introduced to is delightfully real. The children talk and act so naturally that we feel real live children must have sat for their portraits." — *Baltimore Christian Advocate.*

BELLE POWERS'

LOCKET.

"YE ARE THE LIGHT OF THE WORLD."

BY

JOANNA H. MATHEWS,

AUTHOR OF THE "BESSIE BOOKS" AND "THE FLOWERETS."

NEW YORK:
ROBERT CARTER AND BROTHERS,
530 BROADWAY.
1882.

Entered according to Act of Congress, in the year 1871, by
ROBERT CARTER AND BROTHERS,
In the Office of the Librarian of Congress at Washington.

UNIVERSITY PRESS:
JOHN WILSON & SON, CAMBRIDGE.

Dedicated

TO

BESSIE MUIR FISHER.

CONTENTS.

I.	Belle and her Papa	9
II.	An Excitement	25
III.	An Unpleasant Surprise	40
IV.	Sunlight	57
V.	A Day with Maggie and Bessie	73
VI.	Proverb-Pictures	88
VII.	Mabel's New Whim	104
VIII.	The Locket	118
IX.	Belle's Misfortune	133
X.	A Terrible Loss	149
XI.	Belle's Grief	163
XII.	Confession and Repentance	180
XIII.	Mabel's Generosity	196
XIV.	Found	219

BELLE POWERS' LOCKET.

I.

BELLE AND HER PAPA.

DEAR little Belle!
There she sat, upon a low stool, doll and picture-book lying unheeded at her feet, as she watched the slanting beams of light which streamed in between the crimson curtains and poured life and gladness over all within the pleasant room. There she sat, watching them thoughtfully, yet with a half-smile upon her lips, as they travelled slowly and steadily from spot to spot, now over the carpet, now up the table-cloth, now

touching the gilded mirror-frame and making it flash with added brightness, and now falling softly on a vase of lovely flowers and bringing out their brilliant colors in new and more perfect beauty. And now in their noiseless but busy march they fell upon her own little self, the brightest and sunniest thing in all the room, to the loving eyes which watched her.

"What is my darling thinking of?" asked Mr. Powers, breaking the stillness.

In an instant Belle was upon his knee and nestling close to him; but she did not answer his question till it was repeated.

"What were you thinking of, my daughter?" he asked again, laying his hand fondly on the little round head, with its short, dark rings of hair.

"About sunbeams, papa," answered the child, turning her eyes again upon the bar of light, which was now quivering and shimmering among and over the prisms of the chandelier above their heads.

"Ay, they are very pretty," said her father.

"But it was not about *those* sunbeams, papa, though they did make the thinking come into my head. It was about being a sunbeam. I would like to be a little sunbeam, papa."

"And so you may, and so you are, my darling," said the father. "You are papa's little sunbeam, the brightest sunbeam he has on earth; and his way would be very dark and sad without you."

"Yes, papa," said Belle: "you mean I am your comfort, and you are my sunbeam, papa, 'cause you are my comfort; but I was thinking I would like to be a sunbeam to other people too. I wonder if I could. Maggie Bradford says I could."

"I am sure you could, darling."

"Maggie does say such nice things, papa; and so does Bessie; and sometimes when a thing does not seem very pleasant, or as if I would like to do it, they talk about it so that it seems very nice indeed, and so very right that I feel in a great hurry to do it. That is, if I do not feel naughty; for do you know, papa,"—and Belle's voice took a mournful tone,—"do you know sometimes I am so *very* naughty that I feel like doing a thing just because I know I oughtn't. Papa, could you have b'lieved that of me?"

"Yes," said Mr. Powers, smiling: "I could believe that of any one, Belle."

"Could you, papa?" said Belle, solemnly. "Well, that does make me a great relief; for when I used to get good again after I had been so naughty as that, I used to think I must be 'most the wickedest child that ever lived. But one day when I told Maggie and Bessie about it, Maggie said sometimes she felt that way too; and then we made each other promise to keep it a great secret, and never tell anybody."

"And so you keep your promise by telling me," said her father.

"O papa! we didn't mean our fathers and mothers. We don't think you're anybody."

"Thank you," replied her father, taking the compliment as it was meant, though somewhat amused at her way of putting it. "That is right, dear. It is better for little children not to mean their fathers and mothers when they promise not to 'tell anybody.'"

"Yes, papa; and then you see you have nobody but me to tell you secrets, so I would feel too badly not to do it. But I want to know about being a sunbeam, papa; how I can be a sunbeam to 'most everybody, or to a good many people."

"What did Maggie Bradford say about it?" asked Mr. Powers: "let me hear that."

"Why, it was yesterday, when I was spending the day with Maggie and Bessie," answered Belle; "and it was cloudy, and the sun came out from the clouds, and Maggie said — Papa, Maggie is the smartest child; and do you know what I heard Mrs. Norris say about her? She said Maggie had quite a — quite a — a — talent, that was the word, quite a talent for poetry. Are you not very glad, papa, that my in-sep-era-ble has a talent for poetry? Don't you think that is a pretty nice thing for a child to have?"

"Very nice; and I am indeed happy that my Belle has such a talented friend," said Mr. Powers, who knew that he could not please his little daughter more than by joining in the praise and admiration she showered upon her young friends and playmates, Maggie and Bessie Bradford,—"very nice, indeed; but still I do not hear what Maggie said about the sunbeams."

"Well, such a beautiful sunbeam came out of the cloud, papa; and it made every thing look so bright and pleasant, even though the clouds were there yet; and I said if I wasn't myself, I would like to be a sunbeam, 'cause every one was so glad to see it, and it seemed to make things so bright and happy; and then Maggie said we could be ourselves and sunbeams too. Not *really*, true sunbeams, you know, but like sunbeams, to make all bright and glad about us; and she said we did that when we helped each ofer, or when we tried to make sorry people feel glad, and comforted them, or did a kind thing that made some one feel nice and happy. And Bessie and I were very proud of her for saying such a nice thing as that, papa; and we begged her to make some poetry about it, and she made one verse; and then Bessie said she b'lieved we could be sunbeams for Jesus if we chose, and she coaxed Maggie to make another verse about that, and we learned it. Shall I say them to you, papa?"

"Certainly," said her father; and Belle repeated the following simple lines, which she plainly thought extremely fine: —

> "I wish I was a sunbeam,
>   To sparkle all the day;
> And make all glad and happy
>   Who came across my way.
>
> "I'd like to shine for Jesus,
>   And show to every one
> That all my light and brightness
>   Did come from Him, my Sun."

"There, what do you think of that, papa?" she asked in a tone of triumph, which showed her own delight and pride in her little friend's composition.

"I think it very fair for a nine-years-old girl," answered her father.

"I think it is be-ew-tiful," said Belle. "Maggie writes lots and lots of po'try, and she copies it all. Some of it is pious po'try, and she puts that in one book called 'Bradford's Divine Songs,' and she puts the unpious in another called 'Bradford's Moral Poems;' and Bessie and I learn a great deal of them. They're splen-did, and she is just the smartest child,—Bessie says she is."

If Bessie said a thing, it must be so, according to Belle's thinking; and her father did not dispute the fact. Belle went on,—

"And that is the kind of a sunbeam I would like to be, papa, 'cause I s'pose that is the best kind,—to have the light and brightness come from Jesus,—and it would make me nicer and pleasanter to every one."

"Yes, my darling."

"But I don't see how I am to be much of

a sunbeam to any one but you, papa. Maggie and Bessie seem to know how without any one telling them, but I don't know so very well. They are my sunbeams next to you, I know that: are they not, papa?"

"Yes, indeed, my daughter. God bless them," said her father, speaking from his heart as he remembered all that these two dear little girls had been to his motherless child; what true "sunbeams" they had proved to her, cheering and brightening the young life which had been so early darkened by her great loss. Gay, bright, and happy themselves, they were not only willing, but anxious, to pour some of the sunshine of their own joyous hearts into those of others who had not so many blessings.

All this, and more than this, had her young friends done for the lonely little Belle, not only bringing back the light to her saddened eye, and the smiles to her once pitiful face, but also giving her a new interest by awakening in her the wish to shed some happy rays on the lot of others, and leading her by the shining of their own example to become more obedient, gentle, and unselfish than she had ever been before.

"Daphne told me I'll have a whole lot of money when I am a big lady," continued Belle; "and then I should think I could be a sunbeam to ever so many people, and do ever so much to make them glad and happy. I'll build a room, oh, ever so big! and bring into it all the lame and deaf and blind and poor people, and make them have such a nice time. The good ones, I mean: I won't have any naughty people that do bad things. I shan't be a sunbeam to them, or have them in my sunbeam-home; no, nor the disagreeable ones either, who don't have nice manners or be pleasant. I'll take ugly people, 'cause they can't help it; but everybody can be pleasant and polite if they choose, and I shan't help the old things who are not. Ugh!"

"But that is not the way Jesus wants us to feel, dear. When He was here on earth, He taught us that we must try to do good to all, that we might be the children of our Father in Heaven, who, He tells us, 'makes His sun to rise on the evil and on the good, and sendeth rain on the just and the unjust.' Do you know what that means?"

"Um — m — m — yes, papa, I b'lieve so," answered Belle, half unwillingly: "I s'pose it means I ought to try to be a sunbeam to disagreeable people, just the same as if they were pleasant."

"Belle," said Mr. Powers, "do you remember the story Mrs. Rush told you of Lem and Dolly, those naughty, unkind children who treated your little friends so badly; and who were so disagreeable and rude in every way, both in looks and behavior?"

"Oh, yes, indeedy!" answered Belle, in quite a different tone from that she had last used. "I never *could* forget that story; and now I do see what you mean, papa. Maggie and Bessie were sunbeams to poor Lem and Dolly, for all they were so very naughty to them."

"Yes, dear; and they lighted the path to Jesus so that Dolly found the way to Him before she was taken from this world; and by all that we hear it may be that some ray of light has fallen across poor Lem's way too."

"Yes," said Belle, eagerly; "and the ofer day Maggie and Bessie's papa had a letter from the captain of the ship what Lem is a sailor on, and he said he was a real good boy, and tried to do right all he could. But, papa, you see I don't know any very dirty, ragged, horrid children to be a sunbeam to; so what shall I do? I s'pose when I say my prayers I could ask God to let there be some *for* me. I'll ask Him to-night to let there be six dirty beggars, three boys and three girls, that I can be good and kind to, and show the way to Him. Wouldn't that be a good plan, papa?"

"Well, I think I would hardly do that," said her father, smiling. "There is quite enough of misery in the world without asking for more only that we may cure it; and some of it is pretty sure to come in your way. But any little child may in her daily life shed light and brightness around her, even though it does not happen to her to find any such special work as was given to your Maggie and Bessie; and with the will and heart to do it, I think my Belle will be a sunbeam indeed to all with whom she has to do."

Now as you may not know the story of which Belle and her father were speaking, you may like to hear something about it; and you shall have it in a few words.

These two little girls, Maggie and Bessie Bradford, the young friends of whom Belle thought so much, went one summer to spend the season among the mountains; and, while there, fell in with two poor, neglected, and wicked children, named Lem and Dolly Owen. From these children, who seemed to love mischief and wickedness for their own sake, and to feel a spite toward all who were better off than themselves, Maggie and Bessie, and indeed all their family, had much to bear. Every petty annoyance and vexation which they could invent was tried by Lem and Dolly to trouble and grieve those who had never injured them. But although it did cost them a hard struggle, the two dear little girls had forgiven all this, and so won upon the miserable outcasts by the sweet, forgiving kindness they had shown, that the latter were at last brought to look upon them as friends, and to feel sorry for all the evil they had done to them. Nor was this all; for by their simple teachings and bright example they had pointed out to poor, sick Dolly the way to Jesus; and before she died she was led to His feet, and knew that He could save her and take her to dwell with Him. So, happy and trusting, she had gone from a world where she had known little but misery, to that other and better home where sin and suffering never come; while Lem, softened partly by his sister's death, had been put under the care of kind Mr. Porter for a while, and was now, as you have learned from Belle's words, gone as a sailor boy with a prospect and promise of doing well.

All this, and much more which it is not necessary to repeat, — since, if you choose, you may learn all about it in a little book called "Bessie among the Mountains," — had been told to Belle by some of Maggie's and Bessie's older friends; and had, if possible, increased her love and admiration for them. She had received such tenderness and affection from them herself, this motherless little one, and their friendship had brought her such new happiness and comfort, that it was not surprising that she did indeed look upon them as her "sunbeams next to papa," and love them with her whole heart.

Whether Belle and her papa would have talked much more cannot be told, for now they were interrupted by a knock at the door; and when Mr. Powers said, "Come in," a waiter obeyed, bringing a note directed to —

"Miss BELLE POWERS,
Care of her Papa,
In the hottel,
U. S. of America,
New York."

Happily, this note had not gone by post, but had been brought by one servant-man who knew for whom it was intended, and had given it to another, who brought it directly to the young lady whose name it bore. Otherwise, I think it just possible that it might never have reached her.

II.

AN EXCITEMENT.

"THAT is Maggie's writing," said Belle, seizing eagerly upon the note, as the man handed it to her. "I s'pose it's about something nice: Maggie's notes always are,— Bessie's too. Please read it to me, papa."

Mr. Powers did as he was asked; and when Belle had opened the envelope, which was a part of the business she must of course attend to for herself, read aloud these words, written in Maggie Bradford's large, round hand:—

"OH! MY DEAR, DARLING BELLE,— We are so glad Bessie and I are that your papa has made up his mind not to take you away to your home in the south this winter. And not to have you go in that horrid steamer and sail with monsters of the deep and be seasick, which is such a horrible fate that I could not wish it of my worst enemy of which I hope I have none in this world or that which is to come. And because we are so glad about it we wanted to have a public rejoicing, and mamma says we may, and if you don't know what a public rejoicing is it means when people are very glad about something and want other people to be glad too and so they make a great fuss and have something very nice. And so in the present case mamma says you can come and make the public rejoicing with us to-morrow afternoon and Lilly Norris is coming too and Nellie and Carrie Ransom. And mamma is going to let us have a very nice supper and some mottos, of which she knows you are fond as I suppose are all mankind or ought to be if they have any sense, and we think she is the very dearest mamma that ever lived and I hope I shall be her grateful child as I am yours till death and Bessie the same.

"MAGGIE STANTON BRADFORD."

"Oh, yes! I'll go, 'course I will," said Belle, clapping her hands, as her father finished reading the note; and too much accustomed to going and coming to and from Mrs. Bradford's house as she pleased to think it necessary to ask permission. "'Course I'll go. And, papa, isn't this a lovely note? and isn't Maggie just the smartest child to write so nicely? I think she writes just as good notes and letters as big people: yes, I think hers are a good deal more interesting than big people's. And she makes me understand every thing too. I'm glad she told me what a public rejoicing was, 'cause I didn't know before; and isn't that nice and pretty about not going away and monsters of the deep?"

"But you must send your answer: Patrick is waiting," said Mr. Powers.

"Oh! to be sure," said Belle. "Please

write it for me, papa;" and accordingly her father wrote as she dictated: —

"DEAR MAGGIE AND BESSIE, — I guess I will; and I thank you very much for making a public rejoicing, and mottoes and all. Your mamma is so good; and I love her and you, and hope I'll be a sunbeam to everybody. Good-by.

"Your own precious

"BELLE."

On the afternoon of the next day Belle was taken to the home of her young playmates by Daphne, the old colored nurse who took care of her. She was in very good time, you may be sure; for she insisted on going immediately after her own early dinner; and Daphne was too much accustomed to giving her her own way in all things to dream of disputing her wish.

The preparations for the "public rejoicing" were not quite finished, as might have been expected; but that did not much matter where Belle was concerned, for she was so much with the little Bradfords that they looked upon her almost as one of their own family; and she was at once called upon by Maggie to "help with the arrangements," which she was quite ready to do.

"Mamma hasn't had time to buy the mottoes yet," said Maggie, "'cause she couldn't go out this morning; but she is going now and says we are to go with her. Don't you want to come too, Belle?"

Belle was only too glad; and as soon as Mrs. Bradford was ready, the three little girls, Maggie, Bessie, and Belle, set forth with her to make the important purchase.

As they were on their way to the store, Maggie, who had skipped ahead to a corner they had to turn, came running back with face all aglow and eyes full of excitement.

"Oh! mamma!" she said: "there's such a fuss round the corner, and I'm afraid we'll have to pass it."

"What is the trouble?" asked Mrs. Bradford.

"I don't know; but there's a crowd, and I saw a carriage, and a policeman; and there's such a fuss."

"Well," said Bessie, who held the most unbounded faith in policemen, "if there's a policeman, I s'pose he'll fix it all right: won't he?"

"But you see we'll have to pass it to reach the candy-store," said Maggie; "and maybe, it's a drunken man, or a carry-on horse, or an animal escaped out of the menagerie, or a mad dog, or some other dreadful excitement;" and she looked quite distressed as she finished the list of horrors she had imagined.

"I think I can take care of you," said her mother; "and if there should be any danger we will stop in at grandmamma's till it is over."

Thus consoled, but still clinging tight to her mother's hand, Maggie thought they might venture to go on; but as soon as the corner was turned, it became quite plain that there was no danger for them, though there was indeed what she called " a fuss."

In the middle of the street was a carriage about which a crowd had gathered, one of the horses having stumbled, fallen, and broken his leg. On the sidewalk stood a lady in deep mourning, with a nurse, and a child about Bessie's age, the latter screaming at the top of her voice, and dancing up and down, seemingly partly in fear, partly in anger; for she would not listen to her mother and nurse when they tried to soothe her, but struck out her hands passionately at the woman when she tried to draw her away from her mother's side, so that the lady might find opportunity to speak to those about her.

"Oh! the poor little girl! just see how frightened she is," said Bessie.

"I am afraid she is a little naughty, too," said her mother, as the child gave another furious scream and stamped wildly with both her feet upon the pavement; while the lady, who was plainly weak and nervous, drew her hand across her forehead as if the uproar her little daughter was making was almost too much for her.

"But I must speak to the lady and see if I can do any thing for her," continued Mrs. Bradford; and stepping up to her, as she stood a little withdrawn from the crowd, she said kindly, "Can I be of any assistance to you?"

"No, thank you," said the lady: "I am not ill, only startled; and — if Mabel would but be quiet and let me speak and think."

Mabel seemed inclined to do this now that she had caught sight of the other children; for ceasing her loud screams, and standing still, she stared open-mouthed at them.

"My house is but a few steps farther on: will you not come in and rest, and compose yourself?" asked Mrs. Bradford of the stranger.

"No, thank you," she answered again: "I believe we have but little farther to go. Is not the —— Hotel near here?"

"Only a block or two," replied Mrs. Bradford.

"Then we will walk on," said the lady; and directing the nurse to bring some shawls from the carriage, she thanked Mrs. Bradford for her kindness, and taking the hand of her little girl would have gone on.

But this did not please the child, who now drawing sharply back from her mother, said pettishly, —

"No: I want to go to that lady's house and play with those nice little girls."

"But we're not going home. We are going to the candy-store to buy some mottoes," said Belle.

When Mabel heard this, she said she wanted to go to the candy-store and buy mottoes too; and her mother, who, it was plainly to be seen, gave way to her in every thing, said she might do so.

"But if I go and buy you mottoes, will you be a good girl, and come with me to find your uncle and little cousin?" asked the stranger lady.

Mabel promised, anxious now only to secure

the mottoes; and she and her mother and nurse followed Mrs. Bradford and our little friends to the candy-store.

Mrs. Bradford politely waited and let the saleswoman attend to the stranger first, for she saw there would be small chance of peace till the spoiled child had all she desired.

All she desired! There seemed no end to that. Not only Maggie and Bessie, but Belle also, who was accustomed to the most unbounded indulgence, and to have every wish gratified, stood amazed at the number and quantity of dainties which Mabel demanded, and which she was allowed to have. Parcel after parcel was put up for her, till not only her own hands and those of her already well-laden nurse were filled to overflowing, but those of her mother also.

"Now do come, dear," said the latter, when it was impossible that any one of the three could carry another thing: "let us go and see the little cousin, and she shall share them with you."

"No, she shan't," whined Mabel: "I don't want little cousin, and I shan't have her now."

"Well, never mind, then. She is such a nervous child," said her mother, turning to Mrs. Bradford. "She shall not tease you if you do not choose. Come, darling, won't you, with poor mamma?"

But it took so much more promising and coaxing before the unruly child could be persuaded by her weary but foolish mother to go on, that Mrs. Bradford made her purchases and quitted the store with her own little flock, leaving Mabel still whining and fretting, and at the last moment insisting upon having a sugar "Temple of Liberty," which the shop-woman told her was not for sale, but only put there for show.

"That's the spoildest child I ever saw," said Belle, as they turned homewards, each little girl by her own desire laden with a parcel.

"Yes," said Maggie: "she's just the kind

of a child to cry for the moon, and get it too, if she could; but she couldn't. I'm glad," she added, with an air of deep wisdom, "that our parents saw the error of their ways and didn't train us up that way. What are you laughing at, mamma?"

But mamma made no answer; the reason of which Maggie took to be that just at that moment she bowed to a gentleman who was passing; and before she could repeat her question Bessie spoke.

"I'm glad enough I'm not her little cousin she is going to see. I'm sorry for her cousin."

"So am I," said Belle. "I wouldn't have such a cousin as Mabel for any thing. She's too horrid."

"You have a cousin named Mabel, though, haven't you?" asked Maggie.

"Yes, so I have; but then she's not one bit like that Mabel, you know," answered Belle.

"You never saw her, did you?" asked Bessie.

"No, 'cause she lives about a million thousand of miles off, way off in Boston; but she is coming to see me some time," said Belle.

"But if you never saw her, how can you tell she is not one bit like that child?" asked Bessie.

"Why how could she be?" demanded Belle, indignantly: "her mamma is my papa's own sister, and he'd never have such a foolish lady as that for his sister. I guess he wouldn't;" and Belle shook her head in a manner which seemed to say that such an idea was to be put out of the question at once.

"Yes: you know 'birds of a feather flock together,'" said Maggie.

"What does that mean?" asked Bessie.

"Why," answered Maggie, slowly, as she considered how she might make one of her favorite proverbs fit the occasion, "it means — well — it means — that a foolish mother is apt to have a foolish child, and things of that kind. Do you understand, Bessie?"

"Oh, yes!" said Bessie, looking at her

sister with admiring pride: "you always make every thing plain to understand, Maggie. Don't she, Belle?"

"Yes," said Belle: "she's an excellent explainer. And, Maggie, do you know I told papa what nice things you said about being sunbeams, and told him those verses you made; and, oh! didn't he think it was splendid?"

"I don't believe Mabel is much of a sunbeam to her people," said Bessie. "I'm 'fraid her mother don't teach her to be."

"No, indeed, I guess she isn't!" said Belle; "and I wouldn't want to be a sunbeam to her."

"But our Father in Heaven makes His sun to shine on the evil and on the good," said Mrs. Bradford, softly. "Does not my little Belle want to copy Him?"

Just the words her father had used yesterday when she was talking with him on this very subject. They set Belle thinking; and she walked more quietly on towards the house, trying to make up her mind if she could " be a sunbeam" to such a disagreeable child as the one she had just seen.

She had not quite decided when they reached Mrs. Bradford's door, and there for the time her thoughts were taken up with her play and playmates.

But Mrs. Bradford was rather amused when, one of the dolls being supposed to have behaved badly, Belle was overheard to say,—

"This child must be punished severely, she is so very nervous."

III.

AN UNPLEASANT SURPRISE.

THE " public rejoicing " had not nearly come to an end, when, at a much earlier hour than she was accustomed to go home, Belle saw Daphne entering the play-room. Daphne's turbaned head was thrown back, and her lips pursed up in a manner which showed Belle that she was not pleased with something or some one. But whatever might be the cause of the old nurse's displeasure, Belle knew well enough that it would never be visited on her; and Daphne's appearance just at the moment when she was so delightfully engaged did not suit her at all.

"You haven't come to take me home a'ready?" she said.

"But I has, honey: more's de shame," said Daphne, with a look of mingled pity and affection at her little mistress, while a chorus of exclamations arose from all the children.

"I shan't go, now! It's too early," said Belle. "Why, it isn't near dark, Daphne. Did papa send you?"

"S'pose he tinks he did," replied Daphne; "but I specs dere's a new missis come to han', what tinks she's goin' to turn de worl' upside down. 'Pears like it."

"What?" said Belle, not understanding such mysterious hints, yet seeing something was wrong; and Mrs. Bradford asked, "What are you talking about, Daphne?"

"I'se been bidden to hol' my tongue, and I neber talks if I ain't got leave," answered Daphne, with another toss of her turban and several displeased sniffs.

"But you're talking now, only we don't know what it's about," said Bessie.

To this Daphne made no answer, except by closing her eyes in a resigned manner, and giving a sigh which seemed to come from her very shoes.

"I shan't go home, anyhow," said Belle: "the party isn't near out."

"Not when papa wants you, dear?" said Mrs. Bradford, gently.

Belle gave a sigh which sounded like the echo of Daphne's; but she made no farther objection when her nurse brought her hat and prepared to put it on. Daphne clapped on the hat, giving a snap to the elastic which fastened it that really hurt the child, though she was far from intending to do so. Then she seized her in both arms and gave her a loud, sounding kiss.

"You just 'member you allus got yer ole mammy, whatever else you loses, my honey," she said. By this time not only little Belle and the other children, but Mrs. Bradford also, thought something dreadful must have happened; although the latter did know that

Daphne was sometimes foolish, and very apt to make a mountain out of a molehill.

"What's the matter? Where's my papa?" said Belle, in a frightened tone. "Is he lost?"

"He's safe to de hotel, dear," said Daphne. She never condescended to say home: "home" was far away, down on the dear old Georgia plantation. "He's safe to de hotel; that is, if somebody ain't worrit de eyes out his head or de head off his shoulders. You come along, Miss Belle, 'fore all yer tings is gone to rack an' ruin."

"What is the matter, Daphne?" said Mrs. Bradford.

"I telled yer, missis, I ain't got leave for talk; an' I neber breaks orders, no way. But I'se been forgetten: dere's a letter what Massa Powers send you;" and diving into the depths of her enormous pocket, Daphne produced a note which she handed to Mrs. Bradford. The lady opened and read it; while Belle watched her, fearing some evil. But

Mrs. Bradford smiled and looked rather pleased, and said to Belle,—

"It is all right, darling: run home now; papa has a great pleasure for you."

It would be impossible to express the length and depth of the sniff with which Daphne heard this; but Belle did not notice it, and was now rather in haste to say good-by and to go to her papa.

"I wouldn't say any thing more if I were you, Daphne," said Mrs. Bradford, following them out to the head of the stairs.

"Dear! I ain't said nothin', Missis," said Daphne: "didn't her pa forbid it? on'y some folks is so blin'."

"Who's blind? Not papa?" said Belle.

"It am a kin' of sperit blin'ness I'se speakin' ob, honey," said Daphne. "Talk ob spilin' chillen, indeed! Dere's some what's so bad by natur', you couldn't make 'em no wuss if you tried all de days ob yer life."

With which she disappeared, banging the front door after Belle and herself with a force which told that she was anxious for some object on which she might safely vent her displeasure.

Belle talked and questioned all the way home, but received for answer only the same mysterious and alarming hints; till the child hardly knew whether to believe that something dreadful had taken place, or that she was going home to the promised pleasure.

"Now, Miss Belle," said the foolish old woman, as they crossed the hall on which Mr. Powers' rooms opened, " you min' I ain't goin' for let you be snubbed and kep' under. You come and tell yer ole mammy ebery ting; an' I'll fight yer battles, if de French nusses is got sich fly-a-way caps on der heads."

So she opened the door of their own parlor; and Belle, feeling a little worried and a little cross at the interruption to her afternoon's pleasure, passed in.

What did she see?

Upon the sofa, beside her papa, sat a lady dressed in deep mourning; and upon his knee

— was it possible?— yes, upon papa's knee, in her own proper place, was a little girl, quite at her ease, and sitting as if she had a right and belonged there. And — could it be? — Belle took a second look — it really *was* the child who had been so naughty and shown herself so spoiled. She stood for a moment near the door, utterly amazed, and speechless with displeasure.

Now Belle was what is called a generous child; that is, she would readily give away or share what she had with others; but she was jealous of the affection of those she loved, especially of her papa's. He was her own, her very own: all his tenderness and petting must be for her. She could hardly bear that he should caress even her beloved Maggie and Bessie; and if it chanced that he did so, she would immediately claim a double portion for herself. She was quick and bright too; and now she saw in a moment the cause of all Daphne's mysterious hints and melancholy; and they helped to increase the angry, jealous

An Unpleasant Surprise. 47

feeling in her own heart. Daphne had feared that this naughty, contrary child was coming to interfere with her; and Belle feared it now herself. Indeed, was it not plain enough already? There she was on papa's knee, the seat to which no one but herself had a right; and papa's arm was about her.

"Come here, my darling: come and speak to your aunt and little cousin," said Mr. Powers.

And now Belle spoke, indeed, but without moving one step forward, and with a very different tone and manner from those which her father expected.

"Come off of there!" she said, in a low, deep tone of intense passion. "Come off of there! That's my place, he's my papa; you shan't have him, and I shan't have you. You're not my cousin; I won't have you, bad, bad girl!"

She said this with her face perfectly white with rage, her eyes flashing; and she stood bolt upright, her two little hands clenched and stretched downwards on either side. Then the color came fast and deep, rising to the very roots of her hair; her lips were drawn, and her little bosom heaved.

Mr. Powers knew what this meant. Putting Mabel hastily from his knee, he rose and walked over to Belle. When Belle was a baby, and little more than a baby, she had the naughty habit, when any thing displeased her, of holding her breath until she was almost choked and purple in the face. Other children have this ugly way, which is not only naughty, but dangerous. But Belle's mamma had broken her of this when she was very young; and it was a long, long time since her father had seen her do it.

But it was coming now, and must be stopped at once.

"Belle!" he said sharply, and almost sternly, laying his hand on her shoulder,—"Belle!"

It did seem hard, but it was necessary, and was, Mr. Powers knew, the only way to bring his angry little child to her senses. It was enough. She caught her breath hard, then gave one or two deep sobs, and burst into a passion of tears, at the same time turning and trying to run away.

Poor child! It seemed to her that this was proof of her jealous fears. Papa had never spoken so to her before, and it was all because of that strange child who was coming in her place. So she thought, and only wanted to run away out of sight and hearing.

But her father caught her, took her up in his arms, and now spoke to her in the tenderest tones, covering her wet face with kisses and trying to soothe her.

Belle knew that she had been naughty, oh! very naughty; but she still felt very much injured; and, although after a time her sobs became less violent, she clung tightly to her papa, and kept her face hidden on his bosom; shedding there the tears which brought no healing with them because they came from anger and jealousy, and obstinately refusing to look up or speak to her aunt and cousin.

And yet if Belle had been told but yesterday that she was soon to see this little cousin, she would have been delighted. They had never met before, for Mrs. Walton, Mabel's mother, had been living abroad for many years: the little Mabel had been born there, and there several brothers and sisters had died. Perhaps this last was one reason, though it was certainly no good excuse, that Mabel had been so much indulged.

For some months there had been talk of their coming home, but their appearance just at this time was quite unexpected. Young readers will not be interested in knowing what brought them: it is enough to say that here they were, the steamer having brought them to Boston, whence Mr. Walton had sent on his wife and child, he staying behind to attend to some business.

Mrs. Walton had thought to give her brother an agreeable surprise; and so she had, for he had been longing to see her, and to have her help in the training of his motherless little Belle; but Mrs. Walton and Mabel had not been with him half an hour before he began to think that Belle would do quite as well without the training which Mabel received.

The child had been clamorous to see her young cousin from the first moment of her arrival; but Daphne, unwilling to call her darling from her afternoon's pleasure, had invented one excuse after another, till Mr. Powers had insisted that she should bring Belle.

The jealousy of the old colored nurse, who was already put out at Mabel's wilful, pettish behavior, and the way in which she was allowed to handle and pull about all Belle's toys and treasures, was immediately aroused at the idea that her nursling should be made to yield to the new-comer; and she had shown this in the manner which had awakened a like feeling in Belle the moment the child discovered the cause.

Mrs. Walton was vexed, as indeed she might well be, at the reception which Belle had given to herself and Mabel; but the weak and foolish mother readily excused or overlooked in her own child those very faults which she saw so plainly in her little niece.

At first Mabel had been too much astonished at Belle's outbreak to do more than stand and look at her; but when her cousin's cries were quieted, and she lay still with her face hidden on her father's shoulder, giving long, heaving sobs, she began to whine and fret, and to insist that Belle should be made to come and play with her, and show her a set of carved animals, one of Belle's choicest treasures which Mr. Powers had rescued from her destructive little fingers.

"My dear brother," said Mrs. Walton, "it is indeed time that your child was put under other female management than that of servants. She is quite spoiled, I see."

Here a prolonged sniff, ending in something very like a groan, came from near the door where Daphne still stood: while Belle, feeling that both she and her devoted nurse had been insulted, kicked out indignantly with her little feet.

But her father's hand was on the nestling head; and he said very quietly, pouring oil on the wounded spirits,—

"My Belle and her Daphne could not well do without one another; and Belle is much less spoiled than she used to be. She is a pretty good girl now, thanks to the kind teachings she has had, and her own wish to profit by them. Mrs. Bradford, the mother of her little friends Maggie and Bessie, has been very good to her; so has her teacher, Miss Ashton, and several other lady friends: so that she has not been left lately without proper training, even if her papa and old nurse do indulge and pet her perhaps a little too much. Belle and I are all in all to one another now, and she knows I want her to be a good girl. It is a long, long time since she has had such a naughty turn as this, and I know she is sorry and ashamed."

Ashamed Belle certainly was; but I am afraid she was not sorry, at least not truly sorry, for she was quite determined not to look up or speak to her aunt and cousin; and she nursed the angry feelings in her little heart, and made up her mind that they were both quite unbearable.

She was the more sure of this when they all went together into the dining-room. Belle was accustomed to go there with her father, and to eat her simple supper while he dined; and indulged though she was, she never thought of fretting or asking for that which he said was not proper for her; but Mabel called for every thing that she fancied, and was allowed to have all manner of rich dainties, her mother answering when Mr. Powers interfered, —

"It don't do to refuse her any thing. She is so nervous and excitable. I have to manage her the best way I can."

Probably Mr. Powers thought the management which fell to the share of his motherless little Belle was better and more profitable than that bestowed upon Mabel, whose mother was always with her.

It was the same thing when they went upstairs again. Mabel wanted to stand in the gallery above, and look down into the great hall below, where were lights, and numbers of people coming and going; and all the pleadings and promises of her tired mother could not persuade her to go on to their room, where the nurse was engaged unpacking.

But her uncle, who was tired of all this wilfulness, soon put a stop to it, by unclasping the little hands which held so obstinately to the banisters, lifting and carrying her to her mamma's room, where he set her down without a word.

Mabel was so unused to such firm interference with her wishes, and was so astonished at it, that she quite forgot to scream or struggle till he had gone away and the door was shut upon her. Then she made up for lost time; but we will leave her and go with Belle.

Her father saw that she was in no mood for

advice or reproof; just now either would only add to her sudden and violent jealousy of her cousin: so he determined to pass over her naughtiness for to-night, and hoped that she would be more reasonable in the morning. She herself said not a single word about what had passed, or about her aunt and cousin, — at least not to her papa; but when Daphne was putting her to bed, both the little one and the old woman found enough to say to one another; Belle telling her nurse how she had met Mabel that day and how the latter had behaved; while Daphne encouraged her to say as many unkind things as she would, and made the most of all Mabel's spoiled, troublesome ways.

Poor little Belle! She could hardly say her prayers that night, and went to bed feeling more unhappy than she had done for many a long day.

IV.

SUNLIGHT.

THINGS were no better the next morning.

Mrs. Walton did not come down to breakfast, but Mabel chose to go with her uncle and cousin. She was in a better humor than she had been the night before, and would willingly have made friends with Belle if the latter would have allowed her to do so. She was less unruly and wilful at the table also; for after the way in which her uncle had compelled her to obey last night, she was a little afraid of him, and had an idea that he would not allow her to have her own way in the manner her papa and mamma did. She did not like him the less for that though, and when she asked for one or two things which he did not think proper for her, submitted quietly to his refusal, and took what he offered instead. As for Belle, she not only would not speak to her cousin beyond the unwilling "good-morning" which she uttered by her father's orders, but she would not appear to be conscious of her presence at all; never lifting her eyes to her, and if she was forced to turn her face that way, making a pretence of looking over Mabel's head or beyond her. And when they returned to their own parlor, where Mrs. Walton now sat, Belle gathered every toy, book, or other trifle that belonged to her, put them in a closet given for her use, and with some difficulty turned the key and took it out; then planted herself with her back against the door, as if she thought the lock not enough to keep Mabel's hands from her treasures, standing there with a look of the most determined obstinacy and sullenness.

Such behavior was not at all like Belle, and her papa scarcely knew what to make of it. Even in her most wilful days she had never shown herself selfish or sulky; and knowing that she now felt herself aggrieved and injured by Mabel's presence, and fearing to excite fresh jealousy, he did not know how to deal with her.

As for the little girl herself, — no matter how much of all this had been caused by old Daphne, — Belle knew well that she was very naughty; but she determined to persist in that naughtiness so long as Mabel should be there.

To describe Daphne's high-mightiness, not only with Mabel and the French nurse, but also with Mrs. Walton, would be impossible. She carried her turban so straight, and moved and spoke so stiffly, that she almost awed even her little mistress; and Mabel was quite afraid of her. Nor would she give any help or information to the French woman, pretending not to understand her English, which, although broken, was plain enough.

"'Dere ain't no use yer talkin' to me," she said. "I don't unnerstan' yer, nor I ain't goin' to. I'se allus been fetched up 'mong de Peytons, — Miss Belle's mamma she was a Peyton, — an' I'se used to fust-rate English; an' me an' Miss Belle we allus uses it, and neber can unnerstan' no low talk. 'Sides, I'm deaf as a post dis mornin' and can't hear no way."

Daphne was troubled with a convenient kind of deafness, which always came on when she did not wish to hear a thing.

So Mr. Powers, knowing that both Belle and Daphne must be brought to their senses and to better behavior, but not seeing exactly the way to do it without making matters worse, betook himself to his good friend Mrs. Bradford to ask advice.

"What am I to do?" he said when he had finished his story: "if I punish Belle or reprove Daphne, they are in such a state of mind that it will give fresh food for jealousy and bad feeling to both; and yet I cannot let this go on."

"Certainly not," said Mrs. Bradford; "but before we try punishment or reproof, let us see what a little management and kindness will do. Suppose you send Belle, and, if Mrs. Walton will allow it, Mabel with her, to spend the day with my children."

"My sister will allow any thing the child fancies, I fear," the gentleman answered with a sigh; "but you do not know what you are undertaking. A more ungovernable and ungoverned child than my little niece would be hard to find; and I fear that neither you nor your children would pass a pleasant day with Belle and Mabel here, especially if Belle continues in her present mood."

"I do not fear that she will," said Mrs. Bradford. "Maggie and Bessie being of her own age, and having a great sympathy for her, may be able to do more in their simple way to charm the evil spirit than we older people can. As for Mabel, if she will come, she will be under some restraint here, as we are all strangers to her."

"Ah! you do not know her," said Mr. Powers. "I was a stranger to her until yesterday, and yet"— his look and the shrug of his shoulders spoke as strongly as the unfinished sentence could have done.

"Never mind: send her," said the lady. "I will not let her annoy the other children or me *too* much, and I may do her some good."

"Yes," said he, gratefully: "I know that you and yours never shrink from doing good to others because the task may not be an agreeable one. But do you mean to keep a house of correction, or, I should say, of good influences, for all incorrigibly spoiled children?"

"Not exactly," said Mrs. Bradford, returning his smile; "and I believe I have our little Belle more than Mabel in my mind just now; but let them both come, and we will see if we cannot send them back to you this evening in better and happier moods."

Repeating his thanks, Mr. Powers bade her

good-by and went home; where he found that Belle had quitted her stand at the closet-door, Mabel having gone out. For when the latter found that she was not to be allowed to have her cousin's toys, she raised such an uproar as soon as her uncle was out of the way, that her mother promised her every thing and any thing she chose, and had sent her out with the maid to purchase all manner of playthings.

Belle was glad to hear that she was to go to the Bradfords'; and even when she learned that Mabel was to accompany her, she still felt a satisfaction in it, because she was sure that the children would sympathize with her, and be as "offended" with Mabel as she was herself. She was wild to go at once, without waiting for her cousin; and her papa consented that she should do so, hoping that Mrs. Bradford and the children would bring her to a better state of feeling before Mabel made her appearance.

Somewhat to Belle's surprise she found Bessie rather more ready than Maggie to resent her supposed injuries. Bessie did not, it is true, encourage her in her naughty feelings, or in returning evil for evil; but she had been so shocked by Mabel's behavior on the day before, that she could not wonder at Belle's dislike. Moreover, Bessie was a little inclined to jealousy herself; and although she struggled hard with this feeling, and showed it but seldom, she was now ready to excuse it, and find just cause for it, in Belle.

But Maggie was disposed to look at things in a more reasonable light, and to make the best of them.

"Why, Belle," she said, cheerily, "I should think you'd be glad, 'cause now you can be a sunbeam to your cousin, and try to do her good."

"I guess I shan't be a sunbeam to her," said Belle. "I'd be nothing but an ugly, old black cloud, what blows a great deal and has thunder and lightning out of it; and it's just good enough for her."

And at that moment, indeed, little Belle

looked much more like a thunder-cloud than like a sunbeam.

"I just can't bear her. I b'lieve I just hate her, and I'm going to do it too," she continued.

"But that is naughty," said Bessie.

"I don't care: it is truf," said Belle. "I can say the truf, can't I?"

"Well, yes," answered Bessie, "when it's the good truth; but if it's a naughty truth, it's better to keep it in."

"What did Mabel do to you to make you so mad?" asked Maggie.

"Why, she — she" — and Belle hesitated a little, rather ashamed of herself now, as she found how small cause of complaint she really had — "why, she took my things when I didn't say she might. She wanted my carved animals too, what Uncle Ruthven gave me; but papa didn't let her have them, and I wouldn't either. I put them away, and wouldn't let her look at them, — no, not one tiny little peek."

"But, Belle, dear, you don't be selfish with your things gen'ally," said Bessie. "Why won't you even let Mabel see them?"

"'Cause she's too spoiled;" said Belle; "and I b'lieve she'd just go and break them all up. I don't *know* she would, but I b'lieve she would."

"But we oughtn't to b'lieve bad things about people if we don't know 'em," persisted Bessie.

"I shan't let her have my things, anyhow,' replied Belle; "and I'm going to try and have her put out of the country too."

"How can you?" said Maggie. "They have a right to stay here if they want to."

"I'll coax papa to write a letter to the President and ask him to turn out Mabel and her mamma," said Belle; "and I'm going to be very excitable and nervous, so he'll do any thing I want him to."

Maggie had her doubts as to the President's power in such a matter; but she did not make them known, thinking it better to try and soothe Belle's angry feelings, like the wise little peacemaker that she was.

"But I think that we ought to be sorry for your aunt and Mabel, and to have very excusable feelings towards them," she said. "You know they have not had so many advantages as we have, because they have lived abroad for a good many years; and probably they have been corrupted by the fashionable world of Paris."

This was an uncommonly fine speech, even for Maggie; and Bessie and Belle were struck quite dumb by it, and for a moment could do nothing but exchange looks and nods of admiration and wonder; while Maggie, conscious that she deserved their approval, not only for the sentiment, but also for the manner in which it had been expressed, sat gazing serenely out of the window as she received the honors which were due to her.

"Yes, I s'pose so," said Bessie, with a long breath, as she recovered a little.

"I s'pose so too," repeated Belle, in a more amiable tone than she had yet used.

"You see," continued Maggie, thinking it well to strengthen the good impression she had made, and speaking with all the solemn gravity which befitted one who had just uttered such sublime words, — "you see we ought not to be too hard on Mabel, because she is so very saucy and disobedient to her mother that I expect she is one of those to whom the ravens of the valley shall pick out her eye and the young eagles shall eat it. And, children, it is plainly to be seen that it is partly her mother's fault, which is a sad thing, and I fear she will have to bear the consequences. So don't you think we ought to be kind to Mabel and try if we cannot do her some good?"

"Yes," said Bessie, putting her arm about Belle's neck; "and, Belle, maybe when Jesus heard us say we wanted to be sunbeams for Him, He sent this very disagreeable child to be your trial, so He could see if you were quite in earnest about saying it."

This was quite a new view of the subject; and somehow, Belle scarcely knew how, she began to feel more kindly towards her aunt and cousin, and even to have a feeling of pity for them. But the imaginary " six dirty beggars" had taken such strong hold of her mind that she could scarcely resolve all at once to take in their place this well-dressed, well-cared-for, but very naughty little cousin. Mabel could be good and happy if she chose, and Belle did not see why she should be at any trouble to make her so, since nothing but her own wilful humors stood in the way. Still Maggie's words and those of Bessie had already had some influence upon her, and when she next spoke it was in a still milder tone.

"Why, Bessie," she said, "do you really think Jesus had Mabel and her mamma come here just so I could be a sunbeam to them and try to do them good? I don't believe He did."

"Well, maybe He didn't send them here

just for that," answered Bessie; "but when He did send them, I think He'd like you to make a little sunshine for them."

"And then," said fanciful Maggie, always ready to catch at what she thought a poetical idea,—"and then, you know, when the sunshine comes the clouds 'most always go away; so if we try to be very patient and kind with Mabel, maybe the clouds of her crossness and *obstinateness* will roll away and be seen no more."

It was impossible to hold out against such words of wisdom as came from Maggie's lips; and Belle began to feel that here, after all, might be the very opportunity she had wanted.

"And then that would make your aunt glad," persuaded Bessie; "and we are sorry for her."

"Um—m—m, well, I don't know about that," said Belle: "my aunt said a thing about me,—a very disagreeable thing."

"What was it?"

"She said I wanted some kind of management. I forgot what kind. I don't know what word she called it, but it meant something horrid I know; and she oughtn't to say I was spoiled when she spoils her own child."

"No," said Maggie: "people who live in glass houses oughtn't to throw stones; but I fear they generally do, for all."

"What does that mean?" asked Bessie.

"It means when we do a thing a good deal ourselves we oughtn't to speak about other people who do it; but we are apt to."

"Well, then," said Belle, taking the maxim to herself, though Maggie had not meant it for her, "I s'pose if I used to be spoiled myself, I oughtn't to talk so much about my cousin who is."

"But you was never like *that*," said Bessie.

"I used to be pretty spoiled sometimes, and yesterday I was — ugh — I was horrid," answered Belle, a sense of her own past naughtiness coming over her.

"What did you do?" asked Bessie.

"I screamed and hollered — and — and I kicked. I shouldn't be s'prised if my aunt thought I was as naughty as Mabel."

"She that repents ought to make haste to show her repentance," said Maggie. "That is a new proverb I made up on purpose for you, Belle, 'cause I thought it suited you."

"Oh! thank you, Maggie," said Belle: "then I'll do it."

And so our three little girls resolved that they would at least meet Mabel kindly and politely; and as far as possible put the remembrance of her past ill-behavior from their minds.

V.

A DAY WITH MAGGIE AND BESSIE.

MABEL herself had some doubts as to the reception she should meet with if she went to Mrs. Bradford's; and when her mother first proposed it, refused to go. Daphne, who had heard the story from Belle, had not failed to let Mabel know that this lady and her little girls were the friends with whom she had met her cousin yesterday; and had also drawn a very vivid picture of the disgust and dislike with which such behavior as hers was always regarded in their family.

So, as I have said, Mabel at first refused to go near them; but finding it dull in the hotel with only the two nurses for company, as her mamma and uncle had gone out, she changed her mind and declared that she would go to Mrs. Bradford's "to see what it is like, and only stay just as long as I'm a mind to."

"And yer needn't think you'll disappint nobody but yerself if yer come away, little miss," said Daphne, spitefully; for Mabel's new whim did not please her at all, and she would much rather she should have kept to her first decision, and not have bestowed her company where the old woman thought it little desired.

However, she did not dare, much as she would have liked to do so, to refuse to show Mabel and her nurse the way to Mrs. Bradford's house; but she revenged herself by leading them by the longest road and least pleasant way. But this, however much it pleased Daphne, did no hurt to Mabel, since she enjoyed the walk and had no idea of Daphne's object.

"I'se brought you a Tartar," was the old

colored woman's whispered introduction to Mrs. Bradford's nurse when they entered the nursery; and mammy, too, looked askance at the stranger, who immediately perceived that she was not too welcome.

But before she had time to turn about again and say that she would not stay, Maggie came running from the play-room; and putting all shyness and prejudice out of mind, she went up to Mabel, took her by the hand, and said kindly, —

"We have to feel a little acquainted with you before we know you, because you are Belle's cousin; and she is our inseparable. Come into the play-room. You came so late it is 'most time for our dinner, but we will have a good play afterwards."

Such a long, friendly speech to any stranger, even one of her own age, was a great effort for Maggie; but for Belle's sake she wanted to make Mabel comfortable, and put her on her good behavior at once. And she succeeded; for the pout passed from Mabel's lip and the frown from her brow, as she said,—

"Yes, we will; and see what a big box of sugar-plums I have brought. We'll eat them all up."

"If mamma gives us leave; but I am quite sure she will not," said Maggie to herself, and then said aloud,—

"We might play with them, and you shall be the store-woman if you like."

"Yes, so we will," said Mabel. "Didn't Belle try to make you mad at me? She's as mad as any thing at me herself, and won't speak to me, when I never did a thing to her."

"Oh! she's all over that now," said Maggie, wisely noticing only the last part of Mabel's speech. "She and Bessie are putting on the dolls' best suits for you. Come and see them."

And half-ashamed, half-defiant, Mabel followed her little hostess into the play-room to greet Bessie and Belle.

If Mabel was a little shame-faced, Belle was still more so; for she was not accustomed to behave in the way she had done that morning, and her conscience was more tender than Mabel's. But now that she had resolved to do better she would not let shame stand in her way; and going right up to Mabel, she said,—

"Let's kiss and make up, Mabel. I'm sorry I was so cross this morning."

"And will you let me have your playthings?" asked Mabel, as she accepted Belle's offered kiss.

"To look at and play with, but not to keep," answered Belle. "I'll even let you have my carved animals — if you will be careful," she added, determined not to stop half way in her effort to make peace.

And now came mamma, rather expecting to find the little ones awkward and uncomfortable together after all that had passed; but lo! all was peace and sunshine. Her Bessie, it is true, watched the young stranger with serious eyes, and had on her *disapproving* look; for Bessie had been more shocked than it would be easy to tell by Mabel's misbehavior of the day before, and found it hard work to forget it. If Mabel had been some poor, ragged, neglected child, with no one to care for her, and many a temptation in her way, Bessie would have been the first one to make excuses for her, and to say that nothing better could be expected from her; but that any little girl who had loving friends and all manner of comforts and pleasures about her should be so perverse and troublesome, seemed to her out of all reason and hardly to be forgiven.

Still, though she wore her demure little manner, she was very polite to Mabel, and as ready as Maggie to show all her dolls and other treasures. Mabel too, being pleased and amused, was on her good behavior; and all was going smoothly.

Before long the children were called to their dinner. Mabel looked disdainfully at the nice but simple food which was set before them, and refused this, that, and the other thing, saying she did " not like them."

" But you will be hungry before you go home if you do not eat now, my dear," said Mrs. Bradford.

" I'm waiting for something better," said Mabel; at which piece of rudeness all the other children, including even little Frankie, opened their eyes in wonder.

" You will have nothing else except some plain dessert," said Mrs. Bradford.

Mabel pouted, pushed her plate from her, and kicked with her feet upon the legs of her chair; but the lady took no notice, although the three little girls could not help exchanging looks and biting their lips, to express to one another their disapproval of such conduct.

But to Frankie, who was blessed with an uncommonly fine appetite, this refusal to partake of a good meal seemed a most extraordinary and unheard-of thing; so, after staring at her with a pitying look for some moments, and vainly offering her every dainty within his reach, even to "de nice brown stin off my sweet potato," he seemed convinced that she was only naughty, and set about correcting her.

"Did oo ever see Willum what is in 'Slovenly Peter' boot?" he asked.

The only answer he received was a pettish shrug of Mabel's shoulders and a fresh kick upon the chair.

"'Tause he was lite oo, and wouldn't eat his soup," said Master Frankie, with an air of stern reproof; "an' oo will be lite him, an' 'when de fif day tame, alas! dey laid oo in de dround.'"

Which proved too much for the gravity of his little sisters and Belle, who thought this extremely funny; and, in spite of Mabel's scowl, went off into peals of merry laughter.

Mabel hoped and expected that Mrs. Bradford, seeing she would not eat what was set before her, would send for some more dainty and richer food; but she soon found this was not to be, and that the lady did not even appear to trouble herself because she would not eat. This was something quite new to Mabel, who was surprised as well as displeased at Mrs. Bradford's unconcern.

When the dessert was put upon the table, there was a plain rice pudding and a small dish of bright clear jelly.

"I'll take jelly," said Mabel, not waiting till she was asked, as a polite child would have done.

Mrs. Bradford quietly helped each child to a portion of the pudding and some jelly, leaving but little of the latter in the dish.

Mabel eat up her jelly as fast as possible, keeping her eye all the while on what remained in the dish; and as soon as she had finished her own, thrust out her plate, saying, —

"More, please."

Mrs. Bradford gave it to her without a word; but Frankie, encouraged by the applause with which his first reproof had been received, thought himself called upon for another.

Frankie pinned his faith on "Slovenly Peter;" knew it all by heart, quoted from it on all occasions, and drew from it lessons and examples suitable to himself and others.

"Dere's anoder boy named Jatob in 'Slovenly Peter,'" he said severely: "he was so dweedy dat he brote hisself in two. I s'pose you'll be lite him," he added, not at all disturbed by the want of similarity between the two unhappy fates he had predicted for Mabel.

And Mabel felt somewhat abashed when she saw how her greediness had struck this little boy, who she could not but see behaved far better than herself.

"Mamma," said Bessie, "would you rather I should not eat the raisins in my pudding?"

"Well, yes, darling, I think you had better not as you were not very well this morning," said her mother.

Again Mabel was surprised. She knew very well that she would have rebelled against such an order, and had her own way too; but here was this little girl not only submitting quietly and cheerfully to what Mabel looked upon as a hardship, but actually asking if it was her mother's wish. It was something quite new to Mabel.

Had Bessie talked to her for an hour about her greedy, wilful ways, it would not have done one half the good that the example of her own simple regard to her mother's wishes did. And Mabel looked at Bessie, then down upon her plate, then raised her eyes to Bessie's again, with some admiration mingled with the wonder in them; and little Belle, who was watching her cousin, said to herself, —

"Now, I just b'lieve Bessie is a sunbeam, showing Mabel the right, best way to mind her mother; but Bessie don't know she did it."

Quite right, little Belle! And it was not the first ray of light which had fallen that day upon Mabel's wilful and selfish but not hardened young spirit. Already was she beginning to wonder what these children, so obedient and docile, must think of her, and to feel ashamed of her conduct before them.

For some time past a favorite practice of the three little girls,—Maggie, Bessie, and Belle,—had been to draw what they called "proverb-pictures."

This was an invention of Maggie's, and was considered by the children an unfailing source not only of amusement, but also of profit. For all manner of useful hints and gentle moral lessons were supposed to be conveyed in these pictures; and if one noticed any thing in the conduct or speech of another which did not seem exactly proper, she would make a proverb-picture, and kindly present it to the short-comer.

At first a proverb had always been taken as a foundation for these pictures, and Maggie manufactured a good many for the purpose: hence their name; but after a while they were sometimes drawn without reference to any particular maxim or saying, and suited only to the need of the moment.

And I am bound to say that they answered their intended purpose: such hints, if needed, were always taken in good part and seldom neglected; indeed, it was considered rather a treat to receive one, especially from Maggie, and each little girl treasured those which were given to her with great care, and frequently studied them over.

Nor were they considered only as a means of mild reproof or gentle persuasion to do right; but many a little incident and scene of their daily lives were represented, and all these formed to their thinking a very interesting collection.

It is true that the pictures generally needed considerable explanation, not only to other friends who might be treated to a sight of them, but also to one another; but this was really a part of the pleasure, and afforded great satisfaction to the young artists. That is, to Belle and Bessie; Maggie was rather shy about doing this, and preferred to label her pictures, or to write a short explanation beneath.

There could be no doubt that of the three

Belle made the best pictures, indeed they were not bad. for a child of her age; and Maggie and Bessie took much pride in what they considered her great talent, and encouraged her to make the most of it, and put it in constant practice.

So now Maggie bethought herself that it would be well for Belle to try to do her cousin some good by means of these " proverb-pictures." She did not feel intimate enough with her as yet to try to do so herself, but she thought that Belle being such a near relation might very well do it without giving offence.

When they left the table she drew Belle aside and whispered to her: —

" Belle, wouldn't it be a good plan to try Mabel with some proverb-pictures, and see if they will improve her ? You know it's a much agreeabler way of having a good lesson than being scolded or having people mad with you."

" Yes," said Belle: " let's do it now."

" No," said Maggie, " 'cause it would be

stupid for her while we made the pictures; besides, I don't think Bessie and I know her well enough yet, but you might do it when you go home. I composed two proverbs that may do her some good, if you like to take them."

"Yes," said Belle: "tell me 'em, Maggie."

"One is, 'The greedy pig don't get much, after all,'" said Maggie.

"Oh, yes!" said Belle, seeing the beauty of the application at once, and much struck with its force.

"And the other," said Maggie, "is, 'All shun a disagreeable child.'"

"What is shun?" asked Belle.

"To run away," answered Maggie.

"Yes," said Belle, thoughtfully: "those will make very nice pictures, Maggie. I'll take 'em. Say 'em again, 'fear I forget;" and she repeated the new "proverbs" over several times after Maggie, and for the remainder of the afternoon her mind was much occupied with plans for making fine drawings of them for her cousin's benefit.

VI.

PROVERB-PICTURES.

FOR the rest of the day Mabel behaved better, on the whole, than the other children had expected. It is true that she was well amused, and also that being a stranger and company, the other little girls gave way to her, and let her do pretty much as she pleased. She showed herself rather selfish, however, taking all their kindness as a matter of course, and always seizing upon the best and prettiest things for her own use.

But when it was time to go home, and the nurses came for Belle and Mabel, there was much such a scene as had taken place on the day when Mabel had first been met by the other children. She positively refused to go home; and when Mrs. Bradford insisted that she should obey, was led shrieking and screaming from the house, fighting with her long-suffering nurse in a manner which made poor Belle feel "too 'shamed for any thing to go in the street with such disrespectable behavior," and caused Daphne to declare that she and Miss Belle had "never been so *degraced* in all our born days."

This determined Belle to carry out her plan of the "proverb-pictures" as soon as possible; and when her hat was taken off, she immediately begged her papa for a sheet of fool's-cap paper and a pencil, and fell to work.

When Mabel saw what she was about, she wanted to draw also; and her uncle furnished her with paper and pencil.

"What are you making?" asked Mabel.

"I'll tell you by and by, when it's all done," said Belle, severely. "It's not ready for you to understand just yet; but it's going to be a very good lesson for you"

However, she suffered Mabel to look over her paper, and even to copy the figures which grew beneath her busy fingers; Mabel little thinking all the while that she herself was the subject of the pictures. Meantime Mr. Powers and Mrs. Walton, pleased to see the children so quiet, and apparently agreeing so well, talked quietly together.

But this proved too good to last.

"Now they're all done, and I'll tell you about them; and we'll see if they'll improve you," said Belle, when she had completed two pictures. "Do you see these animals?" and she pointed with her pencil to a curious collection of four-legged objects, with every possible variety of tail among them.

"Yes," said Mabel: "what are they? Bugs?"

"No," answered Belle, indignantly: "they are pigs. This is a ' proverb-picture. Prov erbs are meant to do people good, or give them a lesson; but Maggie and Bessie and I think pictures make 'em plainer. This is a proverb that Maggie made up. Here is a man pouring milk into a trough what the pigs eat out of, and this pig," — directing Mabel's attention to a creature without any legs, those four members which were supposed to belong to him lying scattered in all directions over the picture, while long streaks intended to represent floods of tears poured from his eyes, — "and this pig was so greedy that he ran as fast as he could to the end of the trough where he fought the man was going to pour the milk. But the man fought he'd serve him right, and so he went to the ofer end and poured the milk in there; and when the pig tried to run there, his legs were so tired they all fell off; so he couldn't get any milk, and he cried so much he most drowned himself. And the proverb of the picture is, 'The greedy pig don't get much, after all.' When pigs or other people are greedy, their legs gen'ally come off, or other accidents; and if they don't, people think they're very horrid, any way. Do you know who the greedy pig is meant for?"

Mabel had a pretty clear idea, and was not pleased, which was not at all strange; but her curiosity was excited respecting the other picture, and she determined to satisfy it before she made any disturbance.

"What is this picture?" she asked, pouting, but taking no farther notice of Belle's question.

In the second sketch a number of square and triangular bodies, with little, round heads, and long, sprawling legs and arms, were grouped together in the wildest confusion at the two ends of the picture, which extended the whole length of the sheet. In the middle was an object supposed to represent a carriage, the like whereof was never contrived by any coach-maker upon the face of the earth; while a horse, in the same condition as the pig before mentioned,—namely, with all his legs broken off,—lay upon the ground; his mate, looking much like a chair turned upside down, standing by, disconsolate. But the chief interest of the picture was intended to lie in the central figure, in which a small child, with very short skirts and very long limbs, was represented as dancing wildly about, with not rivers, — as in the case of the pig, — but cataracts of tears spouting from her eyes. Two circles, one within the other, stood for her head; the inner one, nearly as large as the outer, being her mouth, stretched to its utmost extent. And lest there should be any mistake as to the likeness, below this figure was printed in large, crooked letters, —

MABURL.

"That," said Belle, more sternly than before, "is a picture about another proverb that Maggie made up on purpose to be of use to you. The name of it is, 'All scamper away as fast as they can go from a spoiled child;' at least, that was what she meant. Here is the spoiled child, squealing and hollering; there is a poor horse that broke his leg; and here are all the people in the street running away from her. These four are policemen, and they were going to take her up; but even the policemen would not stand her, and ran away too. Even her mother 'came degusted at her at last, and left her; so she had not a single person left. And she had no one to give her something to eat, and no one to put her to bed; so she had to sleep in the gutter, and be starved, and in the morning she was dead, and all dirty out of the gutter."

" She wasn't either," said Mabel.

" She was too," contradicted Belle.

Mabel made a snatch at the picture, which Belle as quickly drew from her, so that between them it was torn in two; and Mabel at the same moment set up the shriek she always gave when she was displeased.

Mr. Powers and Mrs. Walton, their conversation thus suddenly brought to an end, turned hastily to see what was the matter.

It was a sorry sight that met their eyes. Belle stood looking at her cousin with a face which, to do her justice, was only intended as the expression of outraged and offended virtue ; while Mabel, shrieking with passion, was frantically tearing to bits the half of the sheet she had secured.

"What is it, children ? What are you quarrelling about now ? " asked both the parents at once.

Mabel did not, perhaps could not, answer ; but Belle spoke up boldly.

"I'm not quarrelling, papa," she said. "I was just trying to give Mabel a lesson of what might happen to her if she didn't behave herself, and she was mad about it; and she tore my picture, — my nice, pretty proverb-picture that I would have given her if she had been good and improved herself by it. I know Maggie and Bessie would think it very interesting if they saw it, and now I can't show it to them ; " and Belle held up the torn sheet with a very aggrieved air. "It was only good intentions, papa ; and she went and wouldn't have 'em," she added, feeling herself almost equal to Maggie Bradford as she made this grand speech.

Even Mrs. Walton could not help smiling in the midst of her efforts to quiet the screaming Mabel and lead her from the room.

When they were gone, Mr. Powers took his little daughter on his knee; but Belle was not satisfied to see that he looked very grave. For a moment or two neither spoke, Belle not knowing exactly what to say, although she did wish to excuse herself; while her father seemed to be thinking.

At last he said, —

"My little girl, how long is this to go on?"

"What, papa?" asked Belle, though she had a pretty clear idea what he meant.

"This constant quarrelling between you and your cousin. Your aunt and I are very glad to see one another again; but all our comfort is destroyed because you and Mabel disagree all the time."

Belle looked rather hurt.

"I'm sure, papa," she said, "I have tried to be good to-day, ever since I went to Maggie's and Bessie's; and she was a little good too, but greedy and selfish. And then she was in such a passion when we had to come home, I fought I'd better try to correct her. And I'm sure I fought proverb-pictures was a good way to do it, but they just made her mad. I s'pose I might have known it," she added, with a sigh: "she is so very bad and spoiled that things that do other children good only make her worse. See, papa, if this wasn't a nice lesson for her;" and spreading out the half of the sheet which she held, Belle explained to her papa the portion of her picture which still remained.

Certainly, Mr. Powers did not find the likeness to Mabel very flattering, or think it calculated to put her in a good humor with herself or the little artist. Nevertheless, he smiled a little, which encouraged Belle, and she went on: —

"I know that child must come to a bad end," she said; "and I shall never try again to be friends with her, or to do her good, — no, never, never!"

"Where is the little girl that wanted to be a sunbeam and shine for Jesus, and show others the way to Him?" asked her father.

Belle hung her head.

"But, papa," she said presently, "you see it's no use with her. I b'lieve she's the wickedest girl that ever lived, and I don't believe there's any thing bad she wouldn't do if she had a chance. She took Baby Annie's chair to-day; and when baby didn't know any better, and cried for it, Mabel wouldn't give it to her. I think I'll just make up my mind to leave her be all the rest of her life, and make b'lieve she isn't my cousin. I wish she stayed to Boston or else to Europe."

"For He maketh His sun to rise on the evil and on the good," said Mr. Powers, softly.

Belle gave another long, despairing sigh, and laid her head back against her father's shoulder; but she made no more attempt to excuse herself or to blame her cousin.

"I will not say that you had not some

thought of doing good to Mabel," said Mr. Powers; "but you began wrong, Belle. I think you did not have very kind feelings in your heart, and that you looked only at what was naughty and perverse in her; and so your picture was not pleasant, and only made her angry. You and Maggie and Bessie understand and love one another, and so you take it pleasantly and patiently when one among you tries this way of helping another in what is right. But I hardly think that any one of you three, good friends as you are, would have been very much pleased to have had such a picture made of you."

Belle sat thoughtful a moment, and then answered,—

"Well, no, papa, I don't b'lieve I would have liked it, if Maggie or Bessie had made a proverb-picture about me slapping Daphne, or being in a passion, or doing any of those very naughty things I used to do so much. But, papa, don't you think my patience about Mabel must be 'most used up?"

"See here," said Mr. Powers, drawing toward him a large Bible which lay near, and turning over the leaves till he found the words he wanted, — "see here, dear, listen to these words: 'Charity suffereth long and is kind, is not easily provoked, thinketh no evil, beareth all things, believeth all things, hopeth all things.' I am afraid my little Belle has not that kind of charity towards her cousin."

"Charity, papa?" said Belle: "charity means giving money and things to beggars and poor people, doesn't it?"

"Charity here means love," said Mr. Powers, — "love to God and to man, that love which makes us want to work for Jesus by being gentle and patient with the faults of others; which will not let us be made angry by little things; which is not ready to think harm of our friends and playmates; love which believes and hopes that even those who are very wrong and naughty may be made better, and which teaches us to take the pleasantest way of doing this, not showing others their faults in a manner to pain or anger them, but trying to show them the better way by an example of kindness and gentleness."

"Um — m — m, no, papa," said Belle, thoughtfully, when her father ceased speaking: "I don't think I have much of that kind of love-charity to Mabel, — no, I don't b'lieve I have."

"I fear not," said her papa; "but will you not try for it, my darling?"

"Yes," she answered; "but you couldn't s'pect it would come very quick, papa. You see I don't know Mabel very well yet, and I guess I don't care 'bout knowing her any more than I do now. She's so very, very spoiled, and I b'lieve she'll never be any better."

"'Charity believeth all things, hopeth all things,'" said Mr. Powers.

"Is that in the Bible Proverbs?" asked Belle.

"No, it is not in Proverbs; but I can give you a verse from Proverbs which may help you: 'A soft answer turneth away wrath.' Wrath means anger."

"Oh, yes!" said Belle: "I found that out; because to-day, when Mabel spoke very angry and cross, Bessie answered her very pleasant and nice; and Mabel looked at her just as if she didn't know what to make of her; and then she spoke nicely too, and quite behaved herself. I s'pose Bessie has love-charity for Mabel. Tell me those words again, papa. I'll learn a little bit of 'em every day till I know 'em all, and try to do 'em too."

Her father did as she asked; and then, for it was growing late, sent her away to bed, satisfied that his lesson was taking root, and that Belle was sorry — though she did not say so — that she had offended Mabel by her "proverb-picture."

He would have been still more sure of this, and well pleased too, had he heard his little girl when Daphne was undressing her, and as usual began to talk of Mabel in a very uncomplimentary way.

"Daffy," said Belle, "I guess we'll have some charity for Mabel, not beggar-charity, but love-charity, that 'b'lieveth all things, hopeth all things,' and makes up its mind maybe she will learn better, and be good, after all."

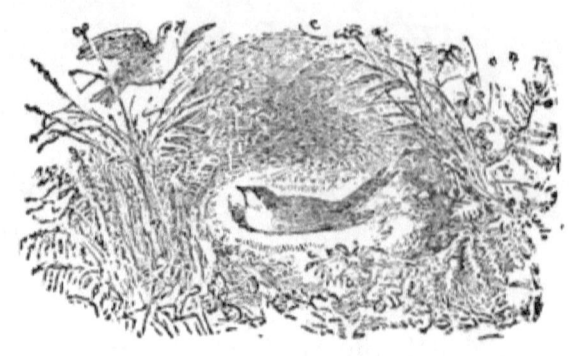

VII.

MABEL'S NEW WHIM.

"PLEASE give me my puf-folio, Daphne," were Belle's first words in the morning before she was up.

"Puf-folio" stood for port-folio in Belle's English; and the one in question was greatly prized by her, as were also the contents. It had been given to her by Harry Bradford, who had also presented one to each of his little sisters; and was formed of large sheets of pasteboard, bound and tied together with bright-colored ribbons; Belle's with red, Bessie's with blue, and Maggie's with purple. To be sure, the binding and sewing had all been done by Aunt Annie; but the materials had been furnished from Harry's pocket-money, and the portfolios were regarded as the most princely gifts, and treasured with great care.

Within were " proverb-pictures " of every variety and in great number, also many a scrap of paper, and—treasure beyond price!—whole sheets of fool's-cap for future use.

One of these last Belle drew forth, and sitting up in her bed began to compose another picture. She was busy with it till Daphne took her up; and even while the old woman was dressing her she kept making little rushes at it, putting in a touch here and there till she had it finished to her satisfaction.

Mabel did not come to breakfast with her uncle and cousin that morning, but chose to take it with her mamma in her own room.

So little Belle, when the meal was over, asked her papa if she might go to her cousin.

"No, dear, I think not," said her father. "You and Mabel are better apart."

"Oh, no, papa!" said Belle; "for I am

going to have love-charity for Mabel, and ask her to have some for me, 'cause maybe I need a little too. I want to make up with her; and here's a new picture for her that I b'lieve she will like better than that old, naughty one I oughtn't to have made last night. Can't I go and be friends?"

Her father examined the picture, to make sure that it could give no cause for new offence; and, satisfied with her explanation, allowed her to go with it to Mrs. Walton's room.

Belle knocked, and being told to come in, obeyed. Her aunt was on the couch, Mabel beside her playing with a doll, and the scowl and pout with which the latter greeted her cousin were not very encouraging.

But Belle, feeling that she had been wrong herself, was determined to persevere in "making up" with Mabel; and she said, though rather timidly,—

"I made you another proverb-picture, Mabel, and"—

"No, no," said Mrs. Walton before she had time to finish her speech: "we have had trouble enough with your 'proverb-pictures,' Belle: you and Mabel cannot agree, it seems; and you had better each keep to your own rooms."

Belle was very much hurt, although she felt this was partly her own fault; and she turned to go with the tears in her eyes.

When Mrs. Walton saw she was grieved, she was sorry for what she had said; and she called to the child, —

"Come here then, Belle: I want to speak to you."

Belle hesitated a moment, holding the door-knob, and twisting it back and forth; but at last she ran over to Mrs. Walton's side, and put her hand in that which was held out to her.

"I'm sorry I teased Mabel, Aunt Fanny," she said; "and I didn't make this picture for a lesson to her, but for a lesson to myself, and to let her see I did want to make up. It's 'most all about me doing things I ought to Mabel; and I'm going to try to have love-charity, and do 'em."

"Let's see," said Mabel, slipping off the couch and coming to her cousin's side, curiosity getting the better of her resentment.

Belle spread out her picture, and explained all its beauties to Mabel.

"That's me, with ugly, naughty lips like I had yesterday, making you," she said; "and I oughtn't to do it when I am often very spoiled myself."

"No," said Mabel, gazing with rapt interest upon the drawing, and already considerably mollified by finding that Belle put her own failings also in her "proverb-pictures."

"But I don't mean to do it any more, Mabel; but just to try to make you be good and love me by living good my own self. And now there's you and me: me letting you have my carved animals, and not being mad even if you broke one a little bit; but you wouldn't if you could help it, would you?"

"No, indeed, I wouldn't," said Mabel, very graciously: "let's be friends again, Belle."

So the quarrel was once again made up, and this time with more good will on both sides.

"You are a dear child," said Mrs. Walton, and she looked thoughtfully and lovingly at the warm-hearted little girl, who, when she knew she had been wrong, was ready to acknowledge it, and to try to make amends; "and Mabel and I should have been more patient with you in the beginning. Poor child! It was a sad thing for you to lose your mother so early."

"Oh! I didn't *lose* her," said Belle, looking up in her aunt's face with eyes of innocent surprise.

"How, dear! What do you mean?" asked Mrs. Walton, wondering in her turn. "Your mamma has gone away from you."

"Yes, but she went to Jesus," answered the child, simply. "You don't lose something when you know it is in a very safe, happy place with some one very dear and good to take care of it, even if you can't see it any more: do you, Aunt Fanny?"

"No, I suppose not," said Mrs. Walton.

"Well, you know mamma has gone to heaven to stay with Jesus, and He's taking care of her; and by and by papa and I will go there too, and then we'll see her again; so we didn't *lose* her, you know. But then I have to be very good and try to please Jesus, and mind what He says; and so I know He wants me to have love-charity for Mabel, and try to not care very much if she does things I don't like. And mamma will be glad too. Oh, no, Aunt Fanny! I didn't lose my dear mamma: I know where she is, all safe."

Mrs. Walton drew her to her and kissed her; while Mabel, wondering at the new softness and sweetness in Belle's face and voice, had forgotten the picture and stood looking at her.

"All safe!"

Five little graves lay side by side in an

English churchyard far away; and of those who rested beneath, the mother had always spoken as her "lost darlings." She never called them so again; for were they not " all safe"? Others had told her the same, others had tried to bring comfort to her grieving and rebellious heart; but from none had it come with such simple, unquestioning faith as from the innocent lips of the unconscious little one before her. Her own loved ones, as well as Belle's dear mother, were not lost, but " all safe."

She kissed the child again, this time with tears in her eyes.

"You see," continued Belle, encouraged to fresh confidence by the new kindness of her aunt's manner, — "you see, Aunt Fanny, that makes another reason for me to try to be good. I have a good many reasons to please Jesus; 'cause dear mamma in heaven would want me to be good, and I would like to do what she wants me to, even more when she is away than if she was here; and 'cause I have to be papa's little comfort. That's what he always says I am, and he says I am his sunbeam too."

"I think I must call you that too, darling. You have brought a little ray of sunshine here this morning."

"Maggie says when we're good it's always like sunshine, but when we're naughty it's like ugly, dark clouds," said Belle. "I'm sorry I was a cloud yes'day, and that other day, Aunt Fanny. But I b'lieve it's time for me to go to school now."

"Do you like school?" asked Mrs. Walton.

"Oh, I guess I do!" said Belle. "Why, you don't know what nice times we have! and Miss Ashton is so kind."

"I want to go to school too," said Mabel.

"Not this morning, dear," said her mother.

"Yes, I shall, — I shall too, now! If Belle goes, I will. I shan't stay here with nobody to play with me."

Mrs. Walton coaxed and promised, but all

to no purpose. Mabel was determined to see for herself the "nice times" which Belle described: school suddenly put on great attractions for her, and nothing would do but that she must go at once. So, taking her by the hand, Mrs. Walton followed Belle to Mr. Powers' parlor, and asked him what he thought of Mabel's new whim.

Now, to tell the truth, Mr. Powers had believed that the best possible thing for Mabel would be to go to school, and be under the firm but gentle rule of Miss Ashton; but he had not yet proposed it to her mother, knowing that the mere mention of it from another person would be quite enough to make the froward child declare she would never go. Therefore he thought well of Mabel's wish, although he was not prepared to take Miss Ashton by surprise on this very morning.

But he knew there was one vacancy in her little school, and that she would probably consent to let Mabel fill it; and he thought it was best to take advantage of the little girl's sudden fancy, or, as Maggie Bradford would have said, to "strike while the iron was hot."

Accordingly he told his sister that he would himself walk to school with the two children, and learn what Miss Ashton had to say on the matter; and Mabel, being made ready with all speed, set forth with her uncle and cousin.

Miss Ashton agreed to take the new-comer; and Mabel was at once put into the seat formerly occupied by Bessie Bradford. Maggie and Bessie had belonged to Miss Ashton's class; but their mother taught them at home now.

Belle could not help a little sigh and one or two longing thoughts as she remembered her dear Bessie who had formerly sat beside her there, but she did not say a word of her regret to Mabel.

Mabel behaved as well as possible during the whole of school-time; whether it was that she was well amused, or that she was somewhat awed by the novelty of the scene, and all the new faces about her, certainly neither Miss Ashton nor Belle had the least cause of complaint against her when the time came for school to be dismissed.

And this good mood continued all that day, with one or two small exceptions. It is true that on more than one of these occasions there might have been serious trouble between the little cousins, but for Belle's persevering good-humor and patience; and she would have thought herself " pretty naughty," if she had behaved as Mabel did. But she excused and bore with her, because it was Mabel for whom she was to have that charity which " suffereth long and is kind."

It was hard work too for little Belle; for, though naturally more generous and amiable than her cousin, she was pretty much accustomed to having her own way in all things reasonable. At home her every wish was law with her papa and nurse; Maggie and Bessie Bradford could not do enough to show their love and sympathy; and all her young playfellows and school-mates followed their example, and petted and gave way to her "because she had no mother." So "giving up" was rather a new thing for Belle, not because she was selfish, but because she was seldom called upon to do it.

However, she had her reward; for, thanks to her own sweetness and good temper, there was peace and sunshine throughout the day. She saw that her father and aunt were pleased with her; and once even Mabel, seeming touched and ashamed when Belle had quietly yielded her own rights, turned around in a sudden and unwonted fit of penitence, and said, —

"There, take it, Belle: you had the best right; and I won't be mean to you again, 'cause you're real good to me."

"My darling has been such a good girl to-day!" said Mr. Powers, as he took her on his knee when they were alone, and she came for the little talk they generally had before her bed-time: "she has been trying to practise the lesson she learned last night, and so has made all about her happy."

"And been a little sunbeam, papa, have I?"

"Yes, indeed, love,— a true sunbeam."

"And did I make you pleased, papa?"

"Very much pleased, and truly happy, dear."

"And mamma will be pleased too, papa; and mamma's Jesus; and it makes Him my Jesus when I try to be His sunbeam and shine for Him, don't it? I guess everybody would be a sunbeam if they always had 'love-charity.' Tell me it over again, papa, so I will remember it very well, and s'plain to me a little more about it."

VIII.

THE LOCKET.

AND this really proved the beginning of better things for Mabel. Not that she improved so much all at once, or that she was not often selfish, perverse, and disobedient; or that she did not often try little Belle very much, and make it hard for her to keep her resolution of being kind and patient. Nor must it be supposed that Belle always kept to this resolution, or that she and Mabel did not now and then have some pretty sharp quarrels; still, on the whole, they agreed better than had seemed probable on their first meeting.

And perhaps it was good for Belle, as well

as for Mabel, that she should sometimes be obliged to give up her own will to another; and there was no fear, while her papa and old Daphne were there to watch over her interests, that she would be suffered to be too much imposed upon.

But there could be no doubt that Mabel was less unruly and exacting. It might be that she was really happier with a companion of her own age, or that she was shamed by Belle's example and kindness to her, or perhaps it was both these causes; but day by day Belle found it easier to be on good terms with her, and the two children were really growing fond of one another.

Other things which had a good effect on Mabel were going to school and being now and then with Maggie and Bessie. She could not but see how much happier and lovelier were those children who were obedient, gentle, and kind; and she learned much that was good without any direct teaching. And even the " proverb-pictures " became to her what they were intended to be to all, a source of improvement; for Maggie understood better than Belle the art of "giving a lesson" without wounding the feelings; and many a gentle reproof or wise hint was conveyed to Mabel by means of these moral sketches, in which she really took a great interest.

After the first novelty of school had worn off, Mabel tired of the restraint and declared that she would go no more; but in the mean time her father had arrived, and he insisted that she should keep on.

For some days after this she gave Miss Ashton a good deal of trouble, and set at defiance many of her rules and regulations; but she soon found that this did her no service, for Miss Ashton, gentle as she was, would be obeyed; and Mabel did not find the solitude of the cloak-room agreeable when she was punished by being sent there, and concluded that, "after all, she had the best time when she was good."

She was not at all a favorite with her school-mates, — this fractious and self-willed little child; and Belle had to "take her part" and coax a good deal before she could persuade them to regard her with any patience, or to feel willing to accept her as a member of their circle.

"What have you there?" asked Mabel one day, coming into Belle's nursery and finding her looking lovingly at some small object she held in her hand.

"It's my locket, — my new locket that papa gave me a few minutes ago," answered Belle.

"Let's see it," said Mabel, making a grasp at it; but Belle was too quick for her, and would not suffer her to seize her treasure.

"You can't have it in your own hands," she said; "for it was my own mamma's, and I don't want any one to touch it, 'cept they loved her. Only Maggie and Bessie," she added, remembering that they had never known her mother, but that she would by no means keep the choicest of her treasures from their hands, feeling sure as she did that they would guard what was precious to her with as much care as she would herself.

"I'll show it to you, Mabel.' Isn't it pretty?" and Belle held up a small locket on a slight gold chain.

It was a little, old-fashioned thing, heart-shaped, and made of fretted gold with a forget-me-not of turquoises in the centre. It was very pretty, — in Belle's eyes, of the most perfect beauty; but its great value lay in that it had belonged, as she told Mabel, to her own mamma when she was a girl.

It was one of Belle's greatest pleasures to sit upon her papa's knee and turn over with loving, reverent fingers the various articles of jewelry which had once been her mother's, and which were to be hers when she should be of a proper age to have them and take care of them. "Mamma's pretty things" were a source of great enjoyment to her; and although Belle loved dress as much as any little girl of her age, it was with no thought

Belle Powers.   p. 122.

of decking herself in them, but simply for their own beauty and the sake of the dear one who had once worn them, that they were so prized. And now and then when her papa gave her some trifle suitable for her, she seldom wore it, so fearful would she be of losing it, or lest other harm should come to it. So now, as things were apt to come to harm in Mabel's destructive fingers, she was very much afraid of trusting the precious locket within them; and stoutly, though not crossly, refused to let her have it.

Mabel begged and promised, whined and fretted; but the locket was still held beyond her reach, till at last she made a dive and had nearly snatched it from Belle's hold.

But Daphne's eye was upon her, and Daphne's hand pulled her back as the old woman said,—

"Hi! dere! none ob dat, Miss Mabel. I ain't goin fur see my ole missus' tings took from my young missus, and me by to help it. I ain't goin fur stan' dat, no way," and Daphne's grasp was rougher than it need to have been as she held back the angry, struggling Mabel.

The child was in a great passion: she struck wildly at the nurse, and screamed aloud, so that her mother came running to see what was the matter.

"There then, never mind," said Mrs. Walton, as Mabel, released from Daphne's hold, rushed to her and complained that Belle would not let her touch her new locket,— "never mind, I will give you something pretty to look at.

"I want a locket like Belle's to keep for my own," said Mabel; "and then I'll never let her see it."

"Pooh! I wouldn't look at it," said Belle, forgetting all her good resolves, "if you showed it to me. I'd just squeeze my eyes tight shut, and never open them till you took it away. And I don't b'lieve the man in the locket-store has any like this."

But Mabel had hardly left the room with her mother before Belle was sorry, as usual, for the anger she had shown, and said remorsefully to Daphne,—

"There now, I went and forgot the Bible proverb papa gave me, and didn't give 'a soft answer' to turn away Mabel's wrath, but just spoke as cross as any thing, and was real naughty. I'll just run after her, and let her touch my locket very carefully with her own hands."

And away she went, ready to make peace, even by doing that which was not pleasant to her; but the dear little thing was only partly successful, for as Maggie afterwards said, when Belle told her the story, "Mabel was of that kind of nature that if you gave her an inch she took an ell;" and no sooner did Belle let her have the locket in her own hands than she wanted to have it about her neck and wear it. This was too much, even for the little peace-maker: she could not make up her mind to give way in this, nor, indeed, could she have been expected to do so; and quiet was not restored till Mabel's mother was worried into taking her out at once in search of such a locket as Belle's.

But the search proved quite fruitless, for no locket exactly like Belle's could be found; and Mabel would not be satisfied with one that was different. In vain did she and her mother go from jeweller's to jeweller's; in vain did Mrs. Walton offer the spoiled child lockets far more showy and costly than the one on which she had set her heart; in vain did the shopman assure her that such as she desired were "quite out of the fashion," an argument which generally went a good way with Mabel: one just like Belle's she would have.

"Then we will have one made," said Mrs. Walton; and inquired when it could be finished. But when the jeweller said it would take a week or more, neither would this satisfy the naughty child, who was in a mood that was uncommonly perverse and obstinate even for her.

"I shall have one to-day," she repeated;

and was so very troublesome that even the patience of her mistaken and spoiling mother at last gave way, and the jeweller heartily wished himself rid of such a noisy, ill-behaved customer.

However, Mrs. Walton gave the order, and promised to bring Belle's locket for the jeweller to see the pattern on Monday, this being Saturday; and then returned home with her naughty child.

Belle had gone out, — gone to Mrs. Bradford's to spend the day with Maggie and Bessie, as she always did on Saturday; and Mabel was left to whine and fret by herself till evening.

This gave her fresh cause of displeasure: she was vexed at her cousin for leaving her alone, and when Belle returned she was greeted with, —

"Mamma is going to take your locket away from you on Monday, and take it to the locket-man to make me one just like it"

"No," said Belle, backing from Mabel to

her father's knee, and holding fast with one hand clasped over the other upon the beloved locket, as if she feared it was to be snatched from her at once.

"You'll let me take it to the jeweller for a pattern, dear: won't you?" said her aunt. "Mabel wants one just like it."

Belle shook her head.

"No, Aunt Fanny," she answered: "I couldn't. It was my own mamma's, and I couldn't let it go from me; and I don't want anybody to have one just like it."

She did not speak unkindly or pettishly, but with a quiet determination in her tone, such as she sometimes showed, and which in some cases might seem to be obstinacy. But it was not so now; and it was evident that the child had some deep and earnest reason for her refusal, — a feeling that the little treasure which had belonged to her mamma had something so dear and sacred about it, that it could not be suffered to pass into strange hands, even for a time; nor could she bear to have it copied.

"The locket-man didn't know my own mamma, Aunt Fanny," she answered again to her aunt's persuasions: "maybe he wouldn't be so very gently with it. I couldn't, — I really couldn't."

Tears gathered in the eyes of the sensitive little one as she spoke, and there was a piteous tremble of her lip which forbade her aunt to urge her farther; but Mabel was not to be so put off.

"You cannot have it, Mabel," said Mr. Powers. "I will not have Belle troubled in this matter."

"What is it?" asked Mr. Walton, looking up from his evening paper, to which he had until now given all his attention, too much accustomed to the fretful tones of his little daughter's voice to pay heed to them when he could avoid it.

The trouble was soon explained; and Mr. Walton, who had lately awakened to the fact that his Mabel had become a most troublesome and disagreeable child, and that it was time for her to learn that she must sometimes give up her own will and consider others, told her that she must think no more of this new whim; and that if she could not be contented with such a locket as he might choose for her on Monday, she should have none at all.

"Then I *won't* have any at all," said Mabel, passionately. "And I won't eat any breakfast or dinner or supper, not for any days."

"Just as you choose," said Mr. Walton, coolly taking up his paper and beginning to read again; while his wife looked pleadingly at him, but to no purpose; and Belle sat gazing in amazement at the child who dared to speak in such a way to her father. Indulgent as Mr. Powers always was to his motherless little girl, she knew very well that he never would have overlooked such disrespect as that, nor could she have believed it possible that she should ever be guilty of it.

Astonishment and indignation at this novel mode of treatment held Mabel speechless and quiet for a moment; then she set up a roar which would have been surprising as coming from so small a pair of lungs, to any one who had not known her powers in that particular.

But here again Mr. Walton, who, as Belle afterwards told her papa, seemed to be disposed to "turn over a new leaf about training up Mabel in the way she should go," interfered, and bade her go from the room, or be quiet.

She chose neither; and the matter ended by her father himself carrying her away, and giving orders that she should be put to bed.

Belle was very sorry for all this, and could not help feeling as if she somehow was to blame, although the matter of the locket was one too near her little heart to be given up. But she went to her uncle when her own bedtime came, and begged that she might go and wish Mabel good-night, and be friends with her once more.

But Mr. Walton thought it better, as did Belle's own papa, that the wilful child should be left to herself till the next day; and he dismissed Belle with a kind kiss, saying, —

"Mabel will feel better in the morning, dear, and then she will be ready to make friends with you; but just now I am afraid she is still too naughty to meet you pleasantly."

IX.

BELLE'S MISFORTUNE.

MR. WALTON was sadly mistaken when he thought that his little girl would have forgotten her ill-temper and be ready to be pleasant and good-humored in the morning. Mabel awoke sulky and pouting, quite determined to believe that Belle had grievously injured her, and obstinately refusing to be reconciled unless she would consent to give up the locket.

Had Belle been willing to do this, her papa and uncle would not have permitted it; but, though Mabel was in a state of displeasure with the world in general that morning, she chose to consider Belle as chief offender, and treated her accordingly.

"But it's Sunday," said Belle, when she refused to kiss her for good-morning.

"Don't I know that?" snapped Mabel.

"But I don't like to be cross with any one on Sunday," pleaded Belle.

"You're cross to me, and so I'll be cross with you,—Sunday and Monday and every day," said the disagreeable child. "Now leave me be."

And Belle, seeing that Mabel was not to be persuaded into a better temper, was forced to do as she said, and let her alone.

And all day, Sunday though it was, Mabel was even more peevish, exacting, and troublesome than usual, till she was a burden and torment to herself and every one about her.

When Monday morning came she was rather more reasonable, but still persisted in being "offended" with Belle, and even refused to walk on the same side of the street with her when they were going to school.

"Will you wear your new locket, Miss Belle?" asked Daphne when she was making her little mistress ready for school.

"No, I guess not," said Belle: "something might happen to it, and maybe it's too nice."

"I reckon it's not too fancy," said Daphne, holding up the locket and looking at it admiringly: "you may wear it if you like, and mebbe Miss Ashton would like to see it."

Now the locket was perhaps not quite a proper thing for Belle to wear to school, and had her father been there he might have advised her to keep to her first decision; but Daphne always liked to deck out her little lady in all the finery she could lay her hands on, and, had she not been held in check by wiser heads, would often have sent her forth to school in very improper guise. And as Mabel was always very much dressed, it chafed Daphne sorely to contrast the simple but more suitable garments of her little Miss Belle with the showy ones worn by her cousin.

So now she persuaded Belle to wear the

locket, saying, not to the child, but to herself, that it "was time folks foun' out her folks was wort somethin', an' had plenty of pretty things if they on'y chose to show 'em;" and, rather against the child's own better judgment, she suffered the nurse to put the locket about her neck.

It was well for Belle, and for those who had the guiding of her, that she was such a docile little girl, generally willing and anxious to do that which she believed to be right, or she might have been sadly injured by the spoiling of her devoted but foolish old nurse. As it was, it did not do her much harm; and Daphne often felt herself put to shame by the little one's uprightness and good sense.

However, on this morning Daphne had her way; and, as I have said, the locket was put on.

As might have been supposed, the new ornament immediately attracted the attention of all Belle's class-mates; and they crowded about her before school opened, to examine and admire, with many an " oh ! " and " ah ! " " how lovely ! " and " how sweet ! "

" Mabel, have you one too ? " asked Dora Johnson ; for the children had found out by this time that if Belle had a pretty thing, Mabel was sure to have one also.

" I'm going to," said Mabel, " one just like it : you see if I don't ; even if that cross-patch won't let the man have it to pattern off of. She thinks herself so great nobody can have a locket like hers."

" Belle's not a cross-patch," said Lily Norris ; " and, Mabel, if you talk that way about her, we won't be friends with you, not any of the class. Belle's old in the class, and you're new ; and we don't think so very much of you. So you'd better look out."

Mabel and Lily were always at swords' points ; for Lily was saucy and outspoken, very fond of Belle, and always upholding her rights, or what she considered such.

" Belle's real selfish," muttered Mabel ; " and you shan't talk to me that way, Lily."

"God gave me my tongue for my own, and I keep it for just what words I choose to say," said Lily, losing both temper and grammar in her indignation; "and Belle's not selfish, but you; and most always when peoples is selfish themselves, they think other ones are that ain't. That's the kind that you're of, Mabel."

"Now don't let's quarrel," said Nellie Ransom, the prudent; "else Miss Ashton will come, and send us to our seats."

"But, Belle, dear," said Dora, "what's the reason you don't want Mabel to have a locket like yours?"

Belle told her story; and very naturally the sympathies of all her class-mates went with her, and Mabel was speedily made to see that she was thought to be altogether in the wrong, which did not tend to restore her to good humor.

"I *shall* take it to the locket-man for a pattern," she said angrily: "you see if I don't. I'll get it, ah-ha."

"No, you won't," said Lily. "Belle knows

you. She'll take good enough care of it; and just you *try* to snatch it now."

What would follow if she did, Lily plainly expressed in the threatening shake of the head with which she accompanied her words.

Farther quarrelling or unkind threats were prevented by the entrance of Miss Ashton, who called her little class to order, and school was opened.

Miss Ashton had more trouble with Mabel that morning than she had had any day since she first came to school. She was pettish and fretful beyond all reason; elbowed and crowded the other children, pouted over her lessons, and was disrespectful to her teacher, and once broke into such a roar that Mrs. Ashton hastily opened the doors between the two rooms and inquired into the cause of the trouble. This soon hushed Mabel's screams; for the elder lady's looks were rather stern and severe, and she at least was one person of whom the wilful child stood in wholesome dread.

But though quiet was restored for a time, it was not to last long; and this seemed destined to be a day of trouble, all through Mabel's naughtiness. Miss Ashton called up the arithmetic class; and as they stood about her desk, she saw Mabel and Lily elbowing one another with all their might, — the former cross and scowling, the latter looking defiant and provoking, and still half good-humored too.

"Children! Lily and Mabel! What are you doing?" she asked.

"Can't Mabel keep her elbow out of my part of the air, Miss Ashton?" said Lily.

"For shame!" said the lady: "two little girls quarrelling about such a trifle as that."

"But, Miss Ashton," pleaded Lily, "she sticks me so! She oughtn't to take up any more room than that;" and she measured with her hand the portion of empty space which according to her ideas rightfully belonged to Mabel; while the latter, conscious that she had been wilfully trespassing, had nothing to say.

"I am sorry that my little scholars cannot agree," said Miss Ashton. "Mabel, stand back a little, and keep your elbows down, my dear. If you cannot behave better, I shall be forced to send you into the other room to my mother; and all the young ladies there will know you have been naughty."

To be sent into Mrs. Ashton in disgrace was thought a terrible punishment; and Miss Ashton had never yet had to put it in practice: the mere mention of it was generally enough to bring the naughtiest child to good behavior, and it was a threat she seldom used. But she knew that the solitude of the cloak-room had quite lost its effect on Mabel, and felt that some stronger measures must be taken if there was to be any peace that day.

Mabel obeyed; but in spite of the threatened punishment, her temper so far got the better of her that she could not resist giving

Lily a parting thrust with her elbow, — a thrust so hard that Lily's slate was knocked from her hand and fell upon the floor, where it broke into three or four pieces.

Now, indeed, Mabel was frightened; and the other children stood almost breathless, waiting for what Miss Ashton would say and do.

She said nothing; what she did was to rise quickly, take Mabel by the hand and turn to lead her to the other room.

Dreading she hardly knew what, Mabel was still too thoroughly terrified at the prospect before her to rebel any farther, or to do more than gasp out, —

"Oh! Miss Ashton! I won't do so any more! I didn't mean to! I will be good!"

Miss Ashton did not answer, but drew her on; when Belle, dropping her own slate beside Lily's, sprang forward and laid her hand on her teacher, looking up with eyes as appealing as Mabel's.

"Please excuse her this time, Miss Ashton," she exclaimed. "I don't think she did mean to break Lily's slate. She only meant to joggle her, and the slate fell out of her hand; but I don't believe she meant to do it. Try her just this once, dear Miss Ashton: maybe she will be good."

Miss Ashton looked down at the little pleader and hesitated. Truth to tell, she had not known how terrible a bugbear her mother was to her young flock: she was sorry now that she saw they had such a dread of her, and perhaps was ready to seize upon an excuse to relent and withdraw her threat.

"Oh! I will, I will be good! I'll never do so any more!" sobbed Mabel.

Miss Ashton turned about, and taking her seat placed Mabel in front of her.

"Very well," she said. "I will excuse you this once; not because you do not deserve punishment, Mabel, but because Belle begs for you. But remember it is for this one time. If you behave again as you have done this morning, I shall certainly punish you. And you must stand there now and say your lesson apart from the other children."

Relieved from the dread of going to Mrs. Ashton, Mabel did not so very much mind that, or the cold, displeased glances of the rest of the class; but as she took her place, she cast a grateful look over at Belle, to whom she truly felt she owed her escape; and Belle felt quite repaid for the "love-charity" which had helped her to forget and forgive Mabel's unkind behavior to herself, and to plead for her.

But the troubles which arose from Mabel's misconduct had by no means come to an end. Belle's place in the class was just at Miss Ashton's left hand, and when she dropped her slate it fell at the foot of the lady's chair. It had escaped the fate of Lily's, not being even cracked by the fall; but as poor little Belle stooped to pick it up, a far worse misfortune than the loss of her slate befell her. As she raised her head, the slight chain about her

Belle's Misfortune. 145

neck caught on the arm of the chair, and the strain snapped it in two.

The sudden check and drag hurt Belle and left an angry red mark about her neck, but she did not heed the sting as she saw chain and locket fall at her feet.

She did not say a word, only snatched it up with a quick, long-drawn breath, and stood for a moment looking at it with the utmost dismay and grief in her countenance; while a chorus of sympathizing exclamations arose from the other children. The mischief done was not so very great, and could easily be repaired; but in Belle's eyes it seemed very dreadful, and as though her treasure was very nearly, if not quite, destroyed. Great tears rose to her eyes and rolled slowly down her cheeks; and she turned to Miss Ashton, piteously holding out the locket in her hand.

Miss Ashton hastened to bring comfort.

"Never mind, dear," she said cheerfully: "it can easily be mended. Tell papa it was an accident, and he will have it done for **you**, I am sure."

"But now the jeweller man will *have* to take it," said Lily, indignantly; "and Belle didn't want to have it go 'way from her, and it's all just for the way Mabel behaved. I should think a broken locket and a broken slate were just about too much consequences of any one's naughtiness and hatefulness for one day."

"Be quiet, Lily," said Miss Ashton.

"But it's true, Miss Ashton: it all came of that old Mabel's badness," persisted Lily.

"Lily, will you be quiet?" repeated her teacher.

Lily dared say no more; but borrowing a slate for the purpose from the child who stood next her, she held it closely before her face, and from behind that shelter made two or three grimaces at Mabel, which, whatever relief they might afford her own feelings, did neither harm nor good to any one else, as they were not seen.

Still Lily's words were felt by Belle and all the rest of the class to be true. Belle's misfortune was certainly the result of Mabel's ill-behavior; and it was very hard for the poor little girl to keep down the angry feelings which seemed as if they would rise up to accuse her cousin.

And Lily's speech or speeches, and the knowledge that she was blamed by all her class-mates, vexed Mabel again, and crushed down the better feelings which had arisen towards Belle, so that she put on an appearance of complete indifference to her distress; and muttered sulkily, —

"I don't care."

"Put the locket carefully away in your desk, dear," said Miss Ashton to Belle, "and do not fret about it. Your papa will have it fixed for you, and it will be as good as ever."

Belle obeyed, putting the locket carefully in one corner of her desk, with a rampart of books raised about it; and then returned to her place, still rather disconsolate, and feeling that she was fully entitled to all the pitying and sympathizing looks bestowed upon her.

After this the business of the class went on without farther interruption, and the arithmetic lesson came to an end.

X.

A TERRIBLE LOSS.

WHEN Miss Ashton dismissed the rest of her little class for the recess which they took in the course of the morning, she told Mabel to come with her; and taking her apart into a room by herself, she talked gravely but kindly to her.

"Would you like it, my dear?" she said, "if I sent you home with a note to your mamma, saying I could no longer have you in the school?"

Mabel hesitated a moment, half-inclined to say that it was just what she would like; but calling to mind the nice plays she often had with her young school-mates, the pretty picture cards she sometimes received from Miss Ashton when she had been particularly good or recited her lessons well, and several other pleasures which school afforded, she thought better of it, and said she would not like it at all; adding to herself what she dared not say aloud to Miss Ashton, that she would carry no such note home, but throw it away in the street if it was given to her.

"And I should be very sorry to do it," said the young lady; "but, Mabel, unless you do better, I cannot have you in my school. Why, my dear, since you have been here there has been more quarrelling and disturbance than during all the rest of the time I have had the class. This must not go on; for you cannot stay with us if you will behave so as to destroy all our peace and comfort."

Mabel hung her head; but she took the reproof better than she generally received any fault-finding; and after Miss Ashton had talked a little more, setting her naughtiness and its sad consequences plainly before her, and urging her to be good and amiable for her own sake as well as because it was right, she had permission to go, and left her teacher, half-repentant, but still not quite determined to take her advice and warnings and make up her mind to be a better child.

In this perverse mood, she did not feel like joining the other children, who were playing on the piazza and out in the garden, but wandered back to the school-room by herself. She sat here a moment or two in her own seat, which was next to Belle's, knocking her feet idly against the floor, and wishing for something to amuse herself with; but still too proud or too sulky to go and play with the others. But presently she bethought herself once more of the locket, and the temptation came to her to open Belle's desk and look at it. Then Conscience whispered, "Shame! shame! Belle was so kind to you, and begged you off when Miss Ashton would have punished you."

The still, small voice made itself heard so

plainly that she could not refuse to listen at first, but she tried to hush it, and at last succeeded.

"I'm not going to do any harm," she said; "only just to look at the locket, and that can't hurt it. Belle won't know it, and she won't be mad."

She opened Belle's desk and peeped in.

There lay the pretty trifle she coveted in the snug corner where the little owner's hands had so carefully placed it. Mabel looked and looked, and from looking she went to touching it. First with only one finger, feeling guilty and ashamed all the time; for with all her faults Mabel was not generally deceitful or meddling. Presently growing bolder, she took it up, shut down the lid of the desk, and sat turning the locket over and over, wishing that the jeweller were there, so that she might show it to him while Belle knew nothing about it.

Suddenly she heard a quick, running step in the hall without; and before she had time to open Belle's desk and put the locket in its place, Dora Johnson came in. Mabel dropped the locket in her lap, and threw her pocket-handkerchief over it. Dora saw nothing wrong, only Mabel sitting there with a very red face, which she supposed to arise from shame, as indeed it partly did, though it came from a cause which Dora never suspected.

"It's beginning to rain, and we all have to come in," said Dora; and the next moment the whole troop of children running in proved the truth of her words. They did not all come into the school-room; but Dora and one or two more were there, so that Mabel did not dare to lift the lid of Belle's desk again and put back the locket.

She was very much frightened, and would have been content, glad indeed, to give up the hope of any locket at all, to have had Belle's safely back where she had left it. She knew that her school-mates would all cry out shame upon her if they saw that she had meddled with the locket, and she knew that she deserved this; but she shrank from the looks and words of scorn and displeasure which she knew would fall upon her when they discovered the treachery she had been guilty of towards her dear little cousin.

So she felt and thought as she sat there with the locket hidden on her lap, and at last feeling that she must rid herself of it by some means, and fearing that Miss Ashton would return to call them to order before she did so, she rose and wandered out of the room, holding the locket fast within her handkerchief.

Most of the children were in the hall, and she went on into the cloak-room. There was no one there; and as she looked about her, wondering what she should do with the locket, the bell rang to call the class back to their places.

With no time to think, with no plan in her head, not meaning to keep the locket from Belle, nor yet seeing her way clearly to the means of getting it back, Mabel hastily dropped it in a corner upon the floor, snatched down her own hat and sacque and threw them over it; then ran back to the school-room with beating heart and crimson cheeks. No one noticed her guilty looks; or, if they did, laid them to the same cause that Dora Johnson had done, and did not speak of them.

The class in reading was now called up; and as Mabel took her stand about the middle of the row, she gave her attention, not to the task before her, but to the locket lying hidden in the cloak-room, and tried to contrive a way out of her difficulty.

Suddenly a thought struck her, and she gave a great sigh of relief. This was the day on which Belle took her music-lesson after school was dismissed: it might be that she would not discover that the locket had been taken out of her desk till she came to go home; and she, Mabel, would have time to put it back after the other children had left.

Miss Ashton's voice roused her, calling back her thoughts to her lesson and reminding her that it was her turn to read; but she did not know where the place was, and when it was pointed out to her by Belle, she stumbled and blundered over words that she knew quite well, and read most disgracefully, finishing her performance with a new burst of crying.

Miss Ashton did not find fault with her, believing perhaps that she really could not help it, but passed on to the next. Would she have taken it so quietly if she had known the true cause of Mabel's excitement? The child could not help asking herself this question, or wondering what punishment she would be called on to bear if her teacher knew all. Not for twenty lockets such as Belle's would she have borne the miserable feelings from which she was suffering now.

So the time dragged on, heavily, heavily, till it was the hour for dismissal; and the little ones prepared to go home.

Mabel watched Belle's every motion, scarcely daring to hope that she would not discover her loss before she went downstairs to her music-lesson; but Belle, never dreaming but that her treasure lay safely hidden in the far corner where she had left it, put books and slate back into her desk in haste, and at last followed Miss Ashton from the room.

Then Mabel hurried into the cloak-room, a new fear taking hold of her, as fears without number or reason ever will of the guilty. Suppose any of the other children had lifted her sacque and found the locket beneath it! No: it lay upon the floor still, — not just as she had left it, it seemed to her fearful, suspicious eyes. But no one turned upon her with accusing words or looks; and she believed herself safe, if she could but manage to be the last child to go.

Nanette, her nurse, who was waiting for her, was too well used to her freaks to be much surprised when she declared she was not going home just yet; and stood by, with what patience she might, to await the pleasure of her hard young task-mistress, who plumped herself down on the floor upon her sacque with a look of dogged determination, which Nanette knew well would change to one of furious passion if she were crossed.

As Lily Norris left the room, she could not refrain from a parting shot at Mabel.

"Mabel," she said, "in the 'Nonsense Book' there is a picture of a sulky girl sitting on a carpet, and the reading about her begins,

> 'There was a young lady of Turkey,
> Whose temper was exceedingly murky;'

and I just b'lieve the man what took her portrait, and made the poetry about her, meant you;" with which, mindful of the fact that Mabel's hand was swift and heavy when she was provoked, she flew from the room, chuckling over her own joke, and joined in her laughter by those who followed her, Lily being considered a great wit.

So had Mabel set all her young school-mates against her that there was scarcely one who did not enjoy a laugh at her expense. But just now Mabel was too much troubled about another matter to vex herself concerning Lily's tantalizing words; and she was only too thankful to see all the children leave the cloak-room one after another.

The moment the last one had disappeared, she ordered her nurse to go out and stand in the entry; sprang to her feet and snatched up the sacque, intending to run with the locket and pop it into Belle's desk without loss of time.

But — there was no locket there!

She shook out her sacque and turned it over and over, looked in her hat, searched all about the corner, and then threw her eyes hastily around the room; all in vain. The locket was certainly gone; and the next moment a cry, half of rage, half of alarm and despair, brought Nanette back to the room.

"What is it?" she asked, seeing by the child's face that it was no ordinary fit of temper that ailed Mabel.

"It's gone! Oh, it's gone!" sobbed Mabel,

wringing her hands and looking the very picture of distress.

"But what is gone? What have you lost?" asked the maid.

Then Mabel recollected herself, and cried less loudly: she would not have even Nanette know how naughty she had been, how meanly she had acted towards the dear little cousin who had been so kind to her; for, mingled with her own fears for herself, there was a feeling of deep remorse for the trouble she had brought upon Belle.

What would the latter say when she should discover her loss?

And, oh dear! oh dear! what was she to do herself?

Even her own indulgent and all-excusing mother could hardly overlook such a thing as this.

She ceased her loud cries and tried to choke back the sobs, but in vain did she wipe her eyes again and again : the tears gathered and rolled down her cheeks as fast as she dried them away; and presently Miss Ashton, who had heard her cries, came running upstairs, followed by Belle, to see what was the matter.

But the moment she saw them, Mabel turned sullen, pouted out her lips, and would not speak; nor could Nanette give any explanation of the cause of the commotion she had made. And Miss Ashton, much displeased at this new disturbance, bade the nurse put on Mabel's things and take her home at once.

Mabel was glad enough to obey, and she suffered Nanette to lead her home as quietly as a lamb, though she could not help a tear and a sigh now and then; and Nanette wondered much what secret trouble should have brought about this distress.

Nor was Mabel's mamma more successful in discovering the cause, when she noticed the traces of tears and observed the child's evident unhappiness. Mabel would not speak, or confess what she had done; and she shrank from her mother's caresses and coaxings, and hung around in sullen, miserable silence, waiting till Belle should come home grieved to the heart, as she knew she would be, by the loss of her much-prized locket.

XI.

BELLE'S GRIEF.

AND meanwhile how was it with little Belle?

Daphne went for her young mistress at the appointed hour, and as soon as the music-lesson was finished took her upstairs to make her ready.

"An' whar's yer locket, honey?" she asked, immediately missing the ornament from about the child's neck.

"In my desk: it did come to a danger, Daphne. I broke the chain and had to put it away. I'm going to bring it, and give it to you to carry home very carefully, so it won't be lost."

"And how did it come broke, dear?" questioned the old woman.

"The chain caught on Miss Ashton's chair and just came right in two," said Belle, refraining from blaming her cousin, upon whom she knew Daphne looked with such an unfavorable eye.

And away she ran into the school-room, Daphne following, and opened her desk.

"Why!" she exclaimed, seeing the locket was not where she had left it; and then hastily fell to turning her books about and looking beneath them.

"What is it, dear heart? Whar am it gone?" said Daphne, seeing no locket, and observing the disturbance of her little charge.

"I don't know; I left it here, — right here in this corner. Oh! Daffy, I know I did; and I never touched it again. Miss Ashton told me not, not till I went home; and I did mind her, oh! I did; but it isn't there. Oh! Daffy, you look, quick. Oh! my locket, mamma's own locket!"

Belle Powers.　　　　　　　　　　　　p. 164.

Daphne turned over each book as hurriedly as Belle had done; then took them all out and shook them, peered within the empty desk, and swept her hand around it again and again; looked on the floor beneath: but all in vain. The locket was certainly not there, and Belle's face grew each moment more and more troubled.

"You's forgot, and took it out again, honey," said the old woman at last.

"Oh! I didn't: how could I forget? And I don't dis'bey Miss Ashton when she tells me don't do a thing. I don't, Daphne; and I couldn't forget about my mamma's locket;" and the poor little thing burst into tears. Such tears!

If any of you have ever lost something which to you was very dear and sacred, which you looked upon as a treasure past all price, and which you would not have exchanged for a hundred pretty things, each one of far more value, you may know how Belle felt at this unlooked-for and, to her, mysterious disappearance of her locket.

"Now, don't yer, honey-pot, — don't yer," said Daphne, vainly trying to soothe her: "'twill be foun', I reckon; but if you ain't took it out, some one else has, for sartain. It ain't walked out ob yer desk widout han's, for sartain sure."

"Oh! but, Daffy, who would take it? who would be so bad to me? They knew I loved it so. I don't b'lieve anybody could tease me so, when they knew it was my own dead mamma's locket," sobbed the little one.

"Um! I spec' it warn't for no teasin' it war done," said Daphne, half hesitating; then her resentment and anger at the supposed thief getting the better of her prudence, she added, "I did allus know Miss Mabel wor a bad one; but I *didn't* tink she so fur trabelled on de broad road as to take to stealin', — and de property ob her own kin too."

The word "stealing" silenced Belle, and checked her tears and cries for a moment or two.

"Stealing!" she repeated; "Mabel wouldn't

steal, Daffy. Oh, that would be too dreadful! She must know better than that. She couldn't *steal* my locket."

"Dunno," said Daphne, dryly: "'pears uncommon like it. Who you s'pose is de tief den, Miss Belle?"

"But we don't have thiefs in our school, Daphne," said the little girl: "we wouldn't do such a thing, and Miss Ashton would never 'low it."

"Dey don't ginerally ask no leave 'bout dere comin's an' goin's," said Daphne: "if dey did, I specs der'd be less of 'em. You 'pend upon it, Miss Belle, dat ar locket's been stealed; an' I can put my finger on who took it right straight off."

"But," persisted Belle, whose distress was still for the time overcome by her horror at Daphne's suggestion, "I don't b'lieve any one would do such a thing; and, Daphne," raising her small head with a little dignified air, and looking reprovingly at the old woman, "I don't b'lieve, either, that it is very proper for you to call Mabel a thief. Maybe she took it to show to the jeweller man, but I know she couldn't steal it. But, oh dear! oh dear! I wonder if I will ever have it back again, my own, own mamma's locket;" and the sense of her loss coming over her with new force, she laid her head down upon her desk and cried aloud.

For the second time the sounds of distress called Miss Ashton to see what the trouble was; and they brought also the older girls from Mrs. Ashton's room, for their recess was not yet quite over. They all crowded about Belle, asking what was the matter, and trying to soothe her; for Belle was a great favorite and pet in the school, partly because she was motherless, — poor little one! — which gave teachers and scholars all a tender feeling toward her, partly because she had many taking and pretty ways of her own, which made her very attractive to every one who knew her.

In her uncertainty and distress the child

could not make plain the cause of her trouble; and Daphne took upon herself the task of explanation, glad, if the truth were known, of the chance. Nor was she backward in expressing her own views of the matter, and in boldly asserting that the locket had been stolen, and she knew by whom.

But at this, Belle roused herself and interrupted her nurse.

"No, no," she said, shaking her head as she looked up with face all drowned in tears, and hardly able to speak for sobbing,—"no, no, Miss Ashton, Daphne *must* be mistaken. Mabel never would do it,—never!"

Now in spite of all her own declarations to the contrary, the fact was that Daphne's repeated accusations, and the recollection of Mabel's threats that she would "have the locket *somehow*," had caused a doubt to enter little Belle's mind as to the possibility and probability of Mabel being the "thief" Daphne called her; but mindful of the "love-charity" she was determined to feel for her cousin,—

the charity which "believeth all things, hopeth all things,"—she tried to put this doubt from her, and to think that some one else was the guilty person, or that the locket had only been taken to tease her. And she was not willing that others should join in Daphne's suspicions and believe that Mabel could do such a thing.

But Miss Ashton herself had too much reason to fear that Daphne's idea was, in part at least, correct. Enough had come to her ears and passed before her eyes, to make her believe that Mabel, in her extreme wilfulness, would not hesitate at any means of gaining her point, especially in the matter of the locket. She did not, it is true, feel sure that Mabel intended to keep the locket; but she thought she had probably taken it against her cousin's will, for purposes of her own; and this was hardly less dishonest than if she had, according to Daphne, *stolen* it outright.

Miss Ashton was very much disturbed. Mabel was proving such a source of trouble, such a firebrand in her little school, which had until now gone on in so much peace and harmony, that she had felt for some days as if it were scarcely best to keep her; still for many reasons she did not wish to ask her mother to remove her.

She thought it better for Mabel to be thrown more with other children than she had hitherto been; and her hope of doing her some good could not be put away readily; and also she shrank from offending and grieving the child's relatives, especially Mr. Powers, who had been a good friend to her mother and herself.

But if Mabel was a child of so little principle as to do a thing like this, it was best to send her away at once, she thought; and there seemed too much reason to fear that it was so.

However, she said nothing of all this to Belle, and when the old colored woman began again, gently stopped her, saying, —

"That will do, Daphne: we will not say any

more about this. Belle, my dear, open your desk and let us search again."

Of course the desk was searched in vain, and not only the desk, but the whole schoolroom; Miss Ashton faintly hoping that Belle might accidentally have pulled the locket out and dropped it on the floor.

Meanwhile the bell had rung to call the older girls back to their class; and Mrs. Ashton, hearing the story from them, came also to Belle to make some inquiries. This was a serious matter, the disappearance of a valuable thing from the desk of one of her little scholars, and needed to be thoroughly sifted. But as soon as she appeared, Belle was seized with that unfortunate dread of the elder lady which possessed all the little girls; and she thought what would become of Mabel if Mrs. Ashton, too, believed her to be a "thief." Visions of squads of policemen, prisons and chains, danced before her mind's eye; and her imagination, almost as quick and fertile as Maggie Bradford's, pictured her cousin dragged away by Mrs. Ashton's orders, while the rest of the family were plunged in the deepest grief and disgrace.

So it was but little satisfaction that Mrs. Ashton gained from her, in reply to her questions. Not so Daphne, however; finding that her young lady gave such short and low answers as could scarcely be understood, she once more poured forth her opinions till again ordered to stop.

However, there was one opinion in which all were forced to agree; namely, that the locket was certainly gone. Belle's sobs were quieted at last, save when a long, heavy sigh struggled up now and then; but her face wore a piteous, grieved look which it went to Miss Ashton's heart to see. With her own hands, she put on the child's hat and sacque, petting her tenderly and assuring her that she would leave no means untried to discover her lost treasure; and then Belle went home with her nurse.

Daphne stalked with her charge at once to

Mrs. Walton's room; and, forgetting her usual good manners, threw open the door without knocking, and standing upon the threshold proclaimed, —

"Miss Walton, Miss Belle's locket am clean gone, chain an' all; an' de Lord will sure foller wid His judgment on dem what's robbed a moderless chile."

Her words were addressed to Mrs. Walton; but her eyes were fastened on Mabel, who shrank from both look and words, knowing full well that Daphne suspected her of being the guilty one.

Mrs. Walton held out her hand kindly to Belle.

"Come here, darling," she said, "and tell me all about it. Your locket gone? How is that?"

Belle told her story in as few words as possible, avoiding any mention of Mabel's naughtiness in school that morning, or of the threats she had used about the locket. She did not even look at Mabel as she spoke, for all the way home the dear little soul had been contriving how she might act and speak so as not to let Mabel see that she had any doubt of her.

"'Cause maybe she didn't take it," she said to herself: "it isn't a *very* maybe, but it's a little maybe; and I would be sorry if I b'lieved she took it and then knew she didn't; and she might be offended with me for ever and ever if I thought she was a thief."

But the puzzle had been great in Belle's mind; for she thought, "If she took it for a pattern for the locket-man and not to keep it, I wonder if it wasn't somehow a little bit like stealing;" and she could not help the suspicion that Mabel had really done this.

Mrs. Walton was full of sympathy and pity, and asked more questions than Belle felt able or willing to answer; but it never entered her mind to suspect her own child.

And, indeed, with all her sad, naughty ways, she had never known Mabel to tell a wilful falsehood, or to take that which did not belong to her in a deceitful, thievish manner. She would, it is true, insist that the thing she desired should be given to her, and often snatch and pull at that which was another's, or boldly help herself in defiance of orders to the contrary; but to do this in a secret way, to be in the least degree dishonest or false, such a thing would have seemed quite impossible to Mrs. Walton.

"Can it be that one of your little classmates is so very wicked?" she said. "Miss Ashton should see to this at once: it is almost impossible that she should not discover the thief if she makes proper efforts."

How did the words of her unsuspecting mother sound to the ears of the guilty little daughter who stood in the recess of the window, half hidden by the curtains, but plainly hearing all that passed as she pretended to be playing with her dolls?

Would Miss Ashton find her out? Would it not be better to go at once and confess?

And it was not only fear for herself which

ed Mabel to hesitate thus: she was really full of remorse and sorrow for the trouble which her wicked, selfish conduct had brought upon Belle; and as she saw how her forgiving little cousin avoided blaming her, these feelings grew stronger and stronger, till they almost overcame the selfishness which ruled her. But not quite; and she resolved to make amends to Belle in some other way.

She thought she was doing this, and showing great generosity, when she came out of her corner, and said to her mother, —

"Mamma, please buy a very nice locket, and let Belle have it 'stead of me. I'll give it up to her, 'cause hers is gone."

Whatever suspicions Belle might have had were at once put to flight by this; but the offer had no charms for her. No other locket could take the place of mamma's; and she shook her head sadly, as she said, —

"No, thank you, Mabel: I don't want any other locket to make up that one. I couldn't wear it, indeed I couldn't."

The melancholy tone of her voice brought back all Mabel's self-reproach, and of the two children she was perhaps really the most unhappy; but still she could not resolve to confess, though Conscience whispered that if she told what she had done, there might be more chance of finding the locket.

Had she not felt too much ashamed and unworthy of praise, she might have been consoled by all that her mother lavished upon her for her offer to Belle. Such unheard-of generosity on Mabel's part was something so new and delightful that Mrs. Walton could not say enough in its praise; and both she and Mr. Walton began to hope that companionship with other children, and Belle's good example, were really doing her good. Little did they think what was the true cause of the proposed self-denial, or of Mabel's evident low spirits.

When Mr. Powers came home, he was almost as much disturbed as Belle to hear of the fate of her locket; and when she had gone to rest that evening, he went to see Miss Ashton to ask if she could take no steps for its recovery.

He was very grave and silent when he came back; and neither that evening nor the next morning did he have much to say concerning it, save that he comforted his little daughter by telling her that he had good hope it would be found.

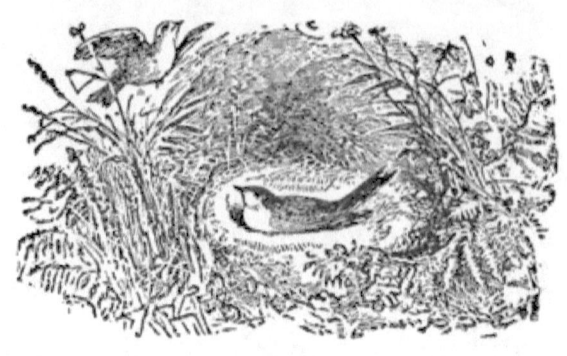

XII.

CONFESSION AND REPENTANCE.

MABEL declared herself not well enough to go to school the next morning; and there seemed some reason to believe it was really so, so dull and spiritless and unlike herself she appeared; and her mother allowed her to remain at home. The true reason was, that she feared to face Miss Ashton and her school-mates.

In vain did her mother try to find out the cause of her trouble, for it was easy to be seen that it was more than sickness.

But the day was not to pass over without Mrs. Walton learning this. For that afternoon Mabel was much startled, and her mother somewhat surprised, by a call from Miss Ashton. Mabel shrank away from her teacher, and said she had to go to her uncle's rooms and play with Belle; and Miss Ashton was not sorry to have her go, as she was about to ask Mrs. Walton to see her alone.

She said this as soon as the child had left the room, adding that she had come on what might prove a painful business; and then told Mrs. Walton all that had passed about the locket on the day before, part of which she had gathered from the other children, part she had known herself. She had reason to fear, she said, that Mabel had taken the locket, as she had threatened to have it, in one way or another; and had been the only one alone in the room with opportunity to take it from Belle's desk. She told, also, how strangely Mabel had acted when she was leaving school the day before; and said, although it might not be so, she could not help thinking that this might be connected with the disappearance of the locket. When Mr. Powers had called upon her the evening before, she told him all she knew, but begged him to say nothing to or about Mabel until she had questioned the other children, and found out who had been in the room beside herself. No one else, so far as she could learn, had been there alone; but the moment Dora Johnson heard that Belle's locket was lost, she had cried out that Mabel must have taken it during recess, and that was the reason she had " acted so queer and mysterious." This was the general opinion among the class, and they were all loud in their indignation against Mabel. She, Miss Ashton, had told them they must not judge too hastily; but she could not herself deny that suspicion pointed very strongly towards the child.

Mrs. Walton was much distressed, but also much displeased, that Miss Ashton, or any one else, should believe Mabel to be guilty. She had never known her to practise deceit or dishonesty of any kind, she said; and insisted on sending at once for the child and questioning her. Miss Ashton did not object, hoping to be able to judge from Mabel's manner whether she were guilty or not; and Mrs. Walton, saying she was determined to hear all that the children had to say on the subject, sent the nurse to bring both Belle and Mabel.

"Is Miss Ashton gone?" asked the latter when the messenger came.

"No, mademoiselle," said Nanette.

"Then I shan't go. I don't want to see her," said Mabel. "Belle, don't go. Stay and play with me."

But Belle, who was very fond of her teacher and always liked to see her, and who, moreover, had a faint hope that she might have brought some good news about the locket, insisted on going to her aunt's room; and Mabel, dreading the same thing and yet not daring to stay behind, reluctantly followed.

Mrs. Walton and Miss Ashton looked from one to the other of the children as they entered; and as the former saw Mabel's downcast, shamefaced look as she came forward, her heart sank within her.

What if Mabel should be really guilty, after all?

"Did you find any thing of my locket, Miss Ashton?" asked little Belle, as soon as she had welcomed the young lady.

"Not yet, dear; but I have some hope of doing so," answered Miss Ashton, looking at Mabel. "Now, I want you to tell your aunt and myself all you can about it. You are quite sure you did not touch it after I saw you put it in your desk?"

"Quite, quite sure, ma'am; and I never went to my desk after that, 'cept to put away my slate; and there's nothing more to tell about it, Miss Ashton, only how I went there to give it to Daphne, and couldn't find it. It was perferly gone," and Belle gave a long sigh, which told how deep her loss lay.

"Mabel," said Mrs. Walton, suddenly, "did you see Belle's locket after it was broken?"

Mabel hung her head more than ever, stammered and stuttered, and finally burst into tears.

Belle looked at her, colored, and hesitated; then stepped up to her, and putting her arm about her shoulder said,—

"I don't b'lieve Mabel did take it, Aunt Fanny: I don't think she could be so mean to me. I *tried* not to b'lieve it, and now I don't think I do. Please don't you and Miss Ashton b'lieve so either, Aunt Fanny."

Belle's "love-charity" was too much for Mabel. Taking her hands from before her face, she clasped them about her cousin's neck, and sobbed out,—

"Oh! I did, Belle. I did take it out of your desk; but I never, never meant to keep it,—no, not even to show to the locket-man; but I couldn't find it to put it back; and I'm so sorry, I'll just give you any thing in the world of mine, 'cept my papa and mamma."

Mabel's words were so incoherent that all her hearers could understand was that she had taken the locket; and though Belle had been obliged to try hard to believe in her cousin's honesty, the shock to the faith she had built up was now so great that her arm dropped from Mabel's shoulder, and she stood utterly amazed and confounded. Mrs. Walton, too, sat as if she were stricken dumb; and Miss Ashton was the first to speak, which she did in a tone more grieved and sorrowful than stern.

"And where is the locket now, Mabel? Did you say you cannot find it?"

Mabel shook her head in assent

"What have you done with it?" asked Mrs. Walton, in a tone that Mabel had never known her mother use to her before.

The whole story was at last drawn from the child, accompanied with many sobs and tears. Belle put full faith in all she said, and almost lost sight of her own trouble in sympathy for Mabel's distress. Her arm went back about her cousin's neck, and her own pocket-handkerchief was taken out to wipe away Mabel's tears.

But Miss Ashton plainly did not believe her story, and even her own mother was doubtful of its truth; for it was told with so much hesitation and stammering.

Mrs. Walton turned to Miss Ashton, with a look which the young lady hardly knew how to answer, except by one which asked that the children should be sent away again; which was done.

"You do not believe what Mabel says, Miss Ashton?" said Mrs. Walton.

"I do not see how it can be so," replied Miss Ashton: "I do not believe there is a child in my class who is not honest; and they all love Belle too much to think of teasing her in any way. Moreover, I know that not one of them was in the cloak-room from the time of the short recess till they were dismissed; and had any child had the will, I do not see that she had the opportunity, to take the locket."

"But your servants?" questioned the anxious mother.

Miss Ashton shook her head sadly.

"My mother's two older servants have been with us for years," she said, "and are quite above suspicion. The younger one, the colored girl, Marcia, who sometimes waits on the children, and now and then goes into the cloak-room, was not in the house. Her sister was sick, and she had been allowed to go to her for the day. She is not, I fear, strictly honest, and has now and then been detected in picking and stealing; and, although I have never known her to take any thing of much value, there is no saying how far temptation might lead her; but, as I say, she was not at home at the time. I grieve to distress you farther, Mrs. Walton; but I do not see that Mabel's story can be true."

"What do you think she has done with the locket?" asked Mrs. Walton, in a trembling voice.

"How could I tell, my dear madam?" replied Miss Ashton, looking with pity at the other lady. "It may be that she has really lost it, but in some other way than the one she relates; or it may be — that she has it still."

"Impossible!" said Mrs. Walton; but although she said the word, the tone of her voice told that she did not believe it impossible. "Mabel is a troublesome, spoiled child, I allow," continued the poor mother; "but I have never known her to tell me a deliberate falsehood, and to make up such a story as this."

"I will have the school-room thoroughly searched," said Miss Ashton; "and whether the locket is found or no, we will at least give Mabel the benefit of the doubt, and treat her as if she were not more guilty than she acknowledges herself to be, unless it is proved that she knows more about it than she says;" and then she rose, and, shaking hands with Mrs. Walton, once more said how sorry she was for the trouble she had been obliged to bring her, and went away.

Meanwhile the two children had gone back to Belle's nursery, where that dear little girl set herself to the task of consoling Mabel as well as she might.

But this was a difficult matter. So long as she had her own way, Mabel generally cared little whether or not people thought her a naughty girl; but as she was really pretty truthful and upright, she was now half-heart-broken at the idea of being considered dishonest and deceitful. She could not quite acquit herself of the latter, since she had taken advantage of Belle's absence to do that which she would not have done in her presence, and now she was very much ashamed of it; but this seemed to her very different from telling a falsehood, which she plainly saw Miss Ashton, and her mother too, suspected her of doing.

She threw herself down on the floor of the nursery in a passion of tears and sobs; and when Belle, sitting down by her, begged her not to cry so, answered,—

"I will, I will: they think I told a story, mamma and Miss Ashton do. I can't bear

Miss Ashton,— horrid, old thing! She made mamma think I did. She's awfully ugly: her nose turns up, and I'm glad it does,— good enough for her."

"Oh! Mabel," said Belle, "Miss Ashton's nose don't turn up. It turns down about as much as it turns up, I think. I b'lieve it's as good as ours."

"I shan't think it is," said Mabel. "I'm going to think it turns up about a million of miles. And, Belle, 'cause everybody thinks I took your locket to keep, and told a wicked story about it, I shall never eat any more breakfast or dinner or supper, but starve myself, so they'll be sorry."

Belle was too well used to such threats from Mabel to be very much alarmed at this.

Mabel went on, trying to make a deeper impression.

"I shan't ever eat any more French sugar-plums," then as the recollection of a tempting box of these delicacies came over her,— "'cept only there are three candied apricots in the box papa brought me last night. I'll eat two of them, and give you the other; and then never eat another thing, 'cause nobody believes me; and it is true,—oh! it is."

"I b'lieve you, dear," said Belle. "I don't think you would be so bad to me,—truly I don't."

"Don't you?" said Mabel, turning around her flushed, tear-stained face; "then I'll give you two apricots, Belle, and only keep one myself; and then starve myself. You're real good to me, Belle, and nobody else is. You're the only friend I have left in the world," she concluded in a tragic whisper, as she sat up and dried her eyes.

"I'll try to coax them not to think you did mean to keep it and tell a story about it," said her little comforter.

"Belle, what makes you so good to me, when I was so bad to you?" asked Mabel.

"'Cause I want you to love me, and be good to me too," answered Belle. "And, besides, Jesus don't want us to be good only to people who are good to us. He wants us to be good to people who are bad to us too."

Mabel sat looking at her cousin in some wonder.

"Do you care very much what Jesus wants?" she asked presently.

"Why, yes," said Belle: "don't you?"

"What does He think about me, I wonder?" said Mabel, musingly, without answering Belle's question, which indeed answered itself, as the recollection of some of her cousin's naughty freaks returned to her. But she said nothing about these; for Mabel's speech brought a thought which she hastened to put into words, thinking that it might give the latter some comfort.

"Oh! Mabel," she said eagerly, "He knows all about the locket; and if you do tell the truf, He b'lieves you, and I am sure He's sorry for you too, even if you was a little naughty about it."

It was a pity that the mother and the governess were not there to see the way in which Mabel's face lighted up. They must have been convinced that, however much she had been to blame, the story she now told was true. Guilt could never have worn that look at the thought that the all-seeing Eye read her heart and believed in her innocence.

And if there was any lingering doubt in little Belle's mind, it was cleared away by that look.

"Now I truly know she is not telling a story," she said to herself, "'cause she looks so glad that Jesus knows all about it; and if she had, she would be frightened to think He knew she was so wicked."

"It's nice to think Jesus knows about it and b'lieves you, isn't it?" she said aloud.

"Yes," said Mabel; "and I love Him for it, and I do love you too; and I'll always love you till I'm all starved and dead. Belle, I know you do care what Jesus wants, 'cause you try to be good and kind. I've just a good mind to try too. Maybe if I do, He'll make them find out where that locket went to."

Now perhaps Mabel's two resolutions did

not agree very well the one with the other; but there was no fear that the first would hold good longer than till supper-time, nor was the hope of reward for herself the best motive for the second. But Belle, and perhaps a higher ear than little Belle's, was glad to hear her say this; and indeed it was a token for good. For Mabel was beginning to see the beauty and sweetness of Belle's conduct, and the warmth and light of her example were taking effect on that perverse and selfish little heart. Belle was proving a " sunbeam" to Mabel, though she did not know it herself.

XIII.

MABEL'S GENEROSITY.

IT would be impossible to tell how troubled and disturbed poor Mrs. Walton was by Miss Ashton's story. So was Mr. Walton when he came home and heard it. It was hard to think that their own and only child could be guilty of such a thing; and yet suspicion pointed so strongly towards her that it was almost impossible to believe otherwise. They talked it over between themselves, and with Mr. Powers when he came; and then the children were called, and told to repeat all they knew once more.

Mabel's story was in no way different from

that she had told before, save that it was given with far less hesitation and difficulty, but in no other respect did it vary from the first; and here was ground for hope that it was true.

Belle, too, told her tale with the same straightforwardness and simplicity that she had done before, but it threw no light on what was so dark; and, as she had done from the first, she carefully avoided throwing any blame on her cousin, and concluded in these words, uttered in a pleading voice: —

"Please, papa, and uncle, and Aunt Fanny, don't believe Mabel took my locket to keep: I don't believe she did, not one bit; and I don't want any one else to think she did."

"Why do you think she did not, dear?" asked Mr. Walton.

"First I *tried* not to think she did," said Belle; "and then when I told her Jesus knew if she was telling the truf, she was glad, and felt better about it, so that made me quite sure. If she had hidden it on purpose to keep it, she would be afraid if she thought Jesus knew it."

Her words brought great comfort and new hope to the father and mother.

"Let's all think she didn't do it, unless we have to be very, very sure she did; and please kiss her, and make up with her, Aunt Fanny, 'cause she feels so bad about it," persisted Belle, drawing her cousin forward, as she stood hanging her head, half-sullen, half-shamefaced, and sorrowful at the suspicion she felt cast upon her. "Aunt Fanny, if I had my own mamma here with me, I would feel very dreadful to know she thought I hid something to steal it, and told ever so many stories about it."

Who could resist her?

Not the mother certainly! who, only too glad to believe her child innocent of more than she had acknowledged, put her arms about her and gave her a kiss of forgiveness; while Mabel laid her head against her mamma's shoulder, and cried there such gentle, penitent tears as she had seldom shed before. For the sweeter and kinder Belle was to her, the more deeply repentant she felt for the wrong she had really done her. And not for the matter of the locket alone did she sorrow: she remembered and felt remorseful for many another selfish, unkind act and speech, and she could not but contrast with shame her cousin's conduct with her own.

"Dear, little Belle!" said her uncle: "hers is the charity that 'thinketh no evil.'"

Mr. Walton said this, knowing nothing of the rules by which Belle had lately tried to govern her behaviour to Mabel as well as to others.

"Yes," said Mr. Powers, drawing his little daughter fondly towards him, and kissing her forehead, — "yes, I believe Belle is really trying for that charity which may keep us in love and peace with God and man."

"Papa," whispered Belle, with her arms about his neck, "it used to be real hard not to think Mabel was the spoildest, worst child that ever lived, and that would do all kinds of bad things; and now I don't like to think that about her, or to have other people think so. Is that 'cause I tried to have love-charity for her? Bessie said it was when I told her."

"Yes, darling, I think so."

"And, papa, Maggie said one of her nice, pleasant-sounding things. She said when we were like sunbeams ourselves it made things look bright and good that would look ugly and dark if we were not nice and bright ourselves. Maggie makes sunniness and shinyness herself, and so does Bessie; and they try all they can to think people wouldn't do bad things."

After the children had been dismissed for the night, there was some discussion between their parents whether or no it would be better for Mabel to go to school till the mystery was cleared up; but it was at last decided that there should be no change, and she should **go as usual.**

"If she will," said Mrs. Walton, to which her husband replied, —

"I think, my dear, it is time that Mabel was learning to do what she *must*, and not what she *will*. I fear we have ourselves to blame for much of this trouble, which has arisen from the wilfulness and selfishness we have too long overlooked."

But Mabel was so subdued by her trouble, and by her sorrow for her past misconduct to Belle, that she offered no resistance to going to school the next day, further than to say she did not want to go.

"Oh, yes, dear!" said her father: "there is no reason why you should not."

"I'm afraid the children won't believe me about Belle's locket," she whispered; "and they'll look at me."

"But if you stay away it would seem as if you were really guilty," said Mr. Walton. "I do not think your school-mates will be unkind to you; and if they are, you must bear it as a part of the punishment for your naughtiness to Belle. Mamma and I think it better you should go. If you are innocent, you need not be afraid."

And Mabel, quite broken-spirited, submitted without any of the loud outcries with which she usually met any opposition to her wishes.

"I know that they'll all be mad at me, and point at me, and every thing," she sobbed, as she started for school with Belle and the two nurses.

"If any of them are so bad to you, I will tell them to have 'love-charity;' and if they don't, I won't be friends with them any more, but be very offended with them indeed," said Belle, forgetting that her new rule could work more ways than one, and hold good for others than Mabel. Just now she was so full of forgiving pity and sympathy for her cousin that she thought only of helping her and doing battle in her behalf.

Mabel's fears were well founded, as it proved. She was met with looks askance, and cold words; while Belle was greeted with a more than usual share of affection. And Dora Johnson, who was not very careful of other people's feelings, and was apt to say rather rude and unkind things without much thought, said in a whisper, loud enough for Mabel to hear, —

"Before I'd come to school if I was a locket-thief!"

Belle heard this too, and at once fired up in Mabel's defence.

"Before I would too, and before Mabel would!" she said, her bright eyes flashing with indignation as she took her cousin's hand in a protecting manner; "and because she isn't a thief is the reason she comes; and she only took it out of my desk to look at, and didn't mean to steal it a bit. But somebody else must have: I don't know who. And if everybody don't be friends with her, they needn't be friends with me either; and I won't have 'em, but will be awfully mad with 'em."

Belle's speech was not perhaps very coherent; but it was understood by all, and had its effect. For since *she* believed that Mabel had not the locket, the rest thought that she must have some good reason for her faith; and no more was said in words, though poor Mabel could not but feel that she was curiously and suspiciously gazed at by every child in the school, as if they expected to read her guilt or innocence written on her face. Still, on the whole, matters were not so bad as she had feared they would be. Miss Ashton was as kind and gentle as usual, and, like her own family, seemed to wish to believe her innocent till she was proved guilty; while Belle was more affectionate and patronizing than she had ever been before, and returned with reproachful or defiant looks every cold or scornful glance that fell to Mabel's share. The search of the cloak-room for the missing treasure had proved quite fruitless. Miss Ashton had taken the trouble to have every thing moved from the room, the floor had been thoroughly swept, and even the corners and edges of the carpet turned up; but all in vain. There was no trace of the lost locket; and Miss Ashton and her mother had decided that they could only wait and see what time would do. Whoever had taken it, such a thing could not remain long hidden: it must be discovered and brought home to the guilty child.

So Miss Ashton told Mrs. Walton when she called to see her again on this unhappy matter; and she would not say, though she gave Mabel the benefit of the doubt, that in her heart she believed her to be that child; and the mother could only hope and pray that it might not be so.

Still it was a most uncomfortable and unhappy matter. Such a thing had never happened before in the little school; and it was sad to believe that there was a thief among that young group.

But good was brought out of all this discomfort and unhappiness. The change in Mabel was surprising as well as encouraging.

She clung to Belle, and to Belle's faith in her, in a way that was really touching, and which went far to convince her friends and teacher that she was really innocent of more than she had confessed. And, contrary to her usual custom, she did not try to excuse herself for what she had done, but was truly penitent, and ready to acknowledge that this trouble had arisen from her own fault. If Belle would have taken them, she would have thrust upon her all her own possessions; and now whenever she saw a pretty thing, she wanted it, not for herself, but for Belle, and was constantly begging her papa and mamma to buy this, that, and the other for her little cousin. And as she became more and more unselfish and yielding towards Belle, she became so towards others, and more obedient and docile to her parents; till the self-willed, outrageous, spoiled elf seemed really changing and quieting down into a tolerably well-behaved, reasonable little child.

That she was really repentant and desirous

Mabel's Generosity.

to make amends to Belle, she showed in a very decided manner when her birthday came around, as it did about three weeks after the loss of the locket.

At this time her Grandmamma Walton was accustomed to send her two gold half-eagles; a large sum for a child like Mabel, and which the old lady probably supposed was put away with care, or used to some good purpose But hitherto it had always been frittered away in toys, candies, and so forth, Mabel claiming such and such portions of it to spend when some trifle struck her fancy.

At the time the locket was first lost, her mother had told her that it would be a good thing if she should spend the money which would come on her next birthday on a new one for Belle; and Mabel had readily agreed. But Mr. Walton, knowing nothing of her good intentions, had bought a handsome locket, and given it to Belle to take the place, as far as might be, of the one which was gone. Belle had thanked him prettily, and admired the gift; then gave it to Daphne to put away.

"Where I can't see it, Daffy, 'cause it makes me feel like crying when I think it was not a bit my own mamma's like that other one I lost."

It was in vain that Daphne tried to persuade her to wear it: the child seemed to have a half romantic, but touching sensitiveness on the subject, which could not be overcome.

But Belle now having her uncle's gift, Mrs. Walton told Mabel that she could spend the money in some other way to gratify her cousin; and Mabel thought of first one thing, then another, which she could purchase for Belle.

But she had not yet decided upon any thing when her birthday came, and with it the usual gift from her grandmother. Running into Belle's nursery on that morning, she found her little cousin standing by the side of old Daphne, who, with her hands over her face, was rocking herself to and fro, moaning and crying, while Belle seemed to be trying to comfort her. Near by stood another colored woman, looking troubled also, though not in the deep distress which Daphne showed. In Daphne's lap laid the contents of Belle's little purse and money-box,— pennies, five and ten cent pieces, and so forth.

Mabel stood a moment in wonder at this unusual state of affairs; and then, full of the business which had brought her, broke forth with,—

"Belle! Belle! Make Daphne dress you very quick. Papa is going to take us out to buy something very nice for you with a whole lot of money grandmamma sent me; and then he is going to take us for a nice long drive in the Park, and let us run about and feed the swans and see the animals. Make haste! make haste!"

Belle shook her head sorrowfully.

"I can't leave Daphne, Mabel," she said. "She has a great trouble. Somebody went and did something naughty, and the people thought it was Daphne's boy,"—Daphne's boy was her grandson,—" and they've taken him to prison; but this woman knew it wasn't him, and they say he can come out if he can get a whole lot of money; and this woman came to tell Daphne; but she hasn't money enough, and I haven't either, and papa has gone away to Philadelphia, and won't come back till day after to-morrrow; and what can we do?" and Belle's eyes filled, as she told the story of her old nurse's trouble.

"And won't you come?" said Mabel.

"No, thank you, Mabel: I couldn't."

"Now go, and take yer pleasure, my honey," said Daphne, ever-mindful of her little lady's happiness. "I'll make you ready."

"No, no, Daffy: I couldn't leave you. Oh! I do wish papa was home. He would fix it all, and get poor Peter out of prison. You are real good, Mabel; but I couldn't care much about the very prettiest present if I had to leave Daphne all alone when she is so sorry."

Mabel hesitated, and thought of those two bright golden pieces. Here was a chance to give Belle a real pleasure, if she chose. She knew Belle well enough to feel sure that she would far rather help her old nurse out of this trouble than to have the most beautiful gift for herself; and Mabel believed that any thing might be done with that sum of money, which was her own to spend as she pleased.

But, as we know, Mabel and Daphne had never been, and were not yet, the best of friends; and it was partly Daphne's fault too. She had no faith in Mabel's improvement, and watched with disdainful and unbelieving eyes her little attempts to be less selfish and wilful. And Mabel knew this, and returned the old woman's dislike with all her little might. So how could she resolve to give up her cherished plan for Daphne's relief? To be sure, it would give Belle more pleasure, but it would give far less to herself; and, indeed, she was not quite sure that she did not feel just the least satisfaction in Daphne's trouble.

"It serves her right for being so cross to me all the time," she said to herself; but then came a feeling of shame at the unkind thought, and she was glad that Belle did not know of it.

"Belle would give the money if it was hers, to get Peter out of prison, I know," she thought, nothing doubting that the two half-eagles could do this; "and maybe it would be the best way to show her I do love her, and am sorry for being so naughty to her about the locket. I'll just do it; but I better do it pretty quick or I'll change my mind about it, 'cause I don't want to one bit."

She rushed from the room, leaving Belle to think that she was vexed at her refusal to go out with her; but in two minutes she was back with the gold pieces, which she thrust into Belle's hand, saying, —

"There, Belle, if you would rather take that black boy out of prison than have a pretty present for you and me to play with, you may. I will give you my money for it;

but I don't do it 'cause I love Daphne, not one bit."

It was not a very gracious way of bestowing a favor, it was true; but it was such a piece of unwonted self-denial from Mabel that her hearers were all taken by surprise, and did not know what to say. Belle stood with the gold pieces in her open hand, looking from them to Mabel, and then at Daphne, who was looking amazed and bewildered in her turn.

But now Mrs. Walton appeared.

When Mabel had run back to her mamma's room for her half-eagles, as she took them from her box she told some incoherent story, which Mrs. Walton had not understood, but which speedily brought her after her little girl to see what was to be the fate of the money. There was no knowing what freak might have taken the child.

"I want Belle to take those to bring Daphne's black boy out of prison, mamma; and she seems as if she didn't want to," said Mabel, half-pouting.

Then Daphne understood; and, rising, courtesied to Mrs. Walton, and told her story; ending by saying that she had not known what Miss Mabel meant, and she begged Mrs. Walton's pardon, and she had not thought of taking the child's money: "Bress her heart! an' I didn't desarve it, cos I did take such a scunner at her."

Mrs. Walton seized Mabel in her arms, and covered her with kisses; while she lavished upon her the most extravagant words of praise and admiration. Mabel had expected this when her mother should come to hear of her offer to Daphne; and, more than this, she had been farther helped to make it by the belief that her mother would not let her be a loser.

"But you shall not spend your birthday gift for that, my darling," she said: "perhaps papa can see to it until Uncle Frederick comes home. We will go and ask him, and tell him what a good, generous girl you are."

Far wiser would it have been if Mrs. Walton had let Mabel learn to do good to others by making some sacrifice of her own wishes; but she could not bear to have her darling deprived of the slightest pleasure, on this day of all others. So bidding Daphne take heart till she should see what Mr. Walton said, she took both children with her to tell him the story.

Mr. Walton listened, and then kindly said he would go and find out the truth of the case at once; and if he thought it right, he would give bail for the lad, for that was what was needed.

"But," he said, "if I do this, I should go at once, that Daphne and her boy may not be kept in misery longer than is necessary; and then my little girls must lose their promised morning in the Park. The promise was made to you first: are you both willing to give up this pleasure for Daphne's sake?"

There was no doubt about Belle; but, as Mr. Walton added, "it was Mabel's birthday, and she must decide."

Now indeed Mabel's generosity and self denial were put to the proof, certainly far more than Belle's. The latter loved her faithful old nurse too dearly to hesitate for one instant; and, even had it not been so, the sacrifice was by no means so great for her as for Mabel. The Park with all its attractions was no new thing to Belle: many a drive and ramble had she had there; but to Mabel, who was a stranger in the city, it was not so familiar, and had not yet lost its first charm for her. And she had been so delighted with the thought of passing the morning there! How could she give it up for Daphne?

Her father waited for her answer, and would not let his wife speak when she would have proposed some other plan; Belle watched her with wistful eyes; and she could not make up her mind to the sacrifice. She hesitated, pouted, frowned; and there were all the signs of a coming storm.

"Very well," said her father, gravely. "I had hoped that my Mabel was really learning to care a little for others, but I fear it is not so. It must be as she decides. We will go for our pleasure, leaving Daphne's boy to stay another day in prison, for I have other business to attend to later in the day; or we will give up this little treat to save her and him much suffering. Which shall it be, Mabel?"

"I said she could have my birthday money," whimpered Mabel; "and mamma said I was as generous as any thing."

"Ah! it did not cost you much to give up the money, my child," said her father. "You and Belle have more toys and pretty things now than you know what to do with; but you are not generous enough to give up that on which you have really set your heart."

Mabel looked over at Belle once more, and as she met the beseeching look in her eyes remembered that here was really the chance to show her cousin that she wished to make up for her past unkindness.

She dropped the pocket-handkerchief which she was pettishly twisting into a string, low ered her raised shoulders, and running to Belle threw her arms about her neck, and said, —

"We'll give up the Park, and let papa go to let out Peter, Belle, — so we will. I'll be generous, even if I don't want to."

So it was settled, and Mr. Walton went on his errand of mercy; of which I need say no more than that it was successful, and Peter set free, to the joy of Belle and Daphne.

XIV.

FOUND.

A FORTNIGHT, three, four, five weeks passed away; and still nothing had been seen or heard of Belle's lost treasure. For the first few days the children could talk of nothing else; and it was only Belle's determination to stand fast by her cousin and take her part, that prevented them from treating Mabel with open slights and coldness. Dark looks and cool words would certainly have fallen to her portion, but for Belle; and she knew and felt this, and it is only justice to her to say that she was grateful to Belle accordingly.

But by and by the affair became an old

story, as every thing does in time, and the children ceased to wonder over it; and Mabel, though never much of a favorite, was allowed to come with them and join in their games as usual. Only the little cousins thought much about the locket; Belle still grieving over her loss, and Mabel mourning it almost as much, with a feeling of guilt and shame added to her sorrow for her cousin's sake.

Perhaps nothing could have done Mabel more good than this sense of the wrong she had done her cousin: it made her see how indulgence in selfishness and wilfulness may bring trouble and distress which we never intended or dreamt of in our perverse mood. Moreover she felt abashed whenever she remembered that the most, if not all of her school-mates, and perhaps her teacher too, believed her guilty of even theft. It is not usually good for people to be unjustly suspected; but in this case it did Mabel no harm. It made her less exacting and domineering at school, and the wish to make amends to Belle made her more yielding and unselfish at home. So her old bad habits were somewhat broken in upon, and the praise and credit which she gained from her parents and little cousin were so pleasing to her that they caused her to persevere and try to do still better. It was not the best motive for improvement, to be sure; but it was something gained in the right way; and by and by Mabel came to the discovery that she was really happier when she was good than when she was naughty.

One day when she and Belle were paying a visit to Maggie and Bessie, she gave what the other children considered a very striking instance of improvement. She had brought with her a very beautiful doll, and to this doll little Annie had taken a desperate fancy; but it was not thought safe to trust it to her hold, although she begged for it piteously. Baby though she was, Annie knew that she never obtained any thing by screaming for it; but she pleaded for the doll, which was held beyond her reach, with kisses and many pretty, broken words, till it was hard to resist her; while Mabel was surprised that she did not scream and cry for that which she wanted so much, and could not help thinking that the little one behaved far better than she would have done herself. And at length her heart was moved so that she could refuse Annie no longer, although no one had thought her unreasonable to do so.

"S'pose I sit down here on the rug by Annie, and let her hold it while I watch her very carefully," she said to Nurse, who was vainly trying to divert baby's attention by offering her every thing else proper for her to have.

"I don't know, dear," said Mammy, divided between the wish to indulge her pet, and the fear that the doll would come to harm in Annie's keeping.

"I'll be very careful of it," said Mabel. "Put her down here by me, and I'll teach her how to hold it nicely."

Nurse obeyed, and the baby was made happy; while her little sisters and Belle looked on in pleased surprise at Mabel's novel generosity.

"Mabel," said Maggie, "I'm going to make you a compliment; and it is that I never saw a child improve more than you do 'most every day. I expect one of these days you'll be quite a benefactor."

"I expect she will too," said Belle. "What does it mean?"

"Somebody who is very generous and does a great many kind things for people," said Maggie.

"Then I'm certain you and Bessie are benefactors," said Belle, pronouncing the long word slowly, as if she were not quite sure of it.

"We try to be," answered Maggie, demurely.

"I'm sure you are too, Belle," said Bessie.

"Yes: she just is," said Mabel. "But I s'pose you don't think I am one."

"Um — well — not quite," said Bessie, not wishing to hurt Mabel's feelings, but too truthful to say what she did not think; "but we have great hopes of you, Mabel. We think it was pretty *benefacting* of you to let Baby Annie have your new doll in her own hands. It must have been pretty hard work."

"Yes," said Maggie: "we didn't expect it of you, Mabel; and we're very agreeably disappointed in you."

Praise from her playmates was something quite new and very pleasant to Mabel, and she began to feel pretty well pleased with herself.

"Yes," she said, with an air of superior virtue, "I b'lieve I'm growing pretty good now."

"You oughtn't to say that," said Bessie: "you ought to say, 'Perhaps I am a little better than I used to be, but I hope I'll be better yet.'"

"Why?" asked Mabel, feeling that she was not properly appreciated in her new character.

"Because," answered Bessie, "it is not the

fashion for people to talk about their own goodness. They ought to wait and let other people do it."

"Well," said Mabel, "I'm sure you were doing it; and so why can't I do it too?"

"But it's *yourself*, you know," said Maggie; "and because 'every crow thinks her own young one the blackest,' that is not any reason for her to talk about it."

"Crows caw, not talk, Maggie," said Bessie, the matter of fact.

"Oh, well!" said Maggie, "the lesson out of the proverb is all the same."

"I didn't mean to be proud about it," said Mabel, quite humbly; "but I couldn't help feeling a little nice when I thought I wasn't so naughty as I used to be. Mamma says I am better, and papa says so too."

"And we say so too," said Bessie, kissing her, the first kiss she had ever given her of her own free will; "and we are very glad of it, Mabel."

"I think it was Belle that made me a better

girl," said Mabel: "she was so good to me, I had to be. 'Least she was pretty mad with me at first: wasn't you, Belle? And before I did a thing to her too; but afterwards she was real good to me. And you and Maggie were good to me too; and everybody liked you, so I thought it must be nice to be good, and I would be too. And I b'lieve I do like it better."

"You see example is better than practice," said Maggie, meaning "precept;" "and so 'cause Belle was good and kind herself, that put you in a mind to be so; and that ought to make you very happy, Belle. I find it is very true that if 'evil communications corrupt good manners,' good communications also corrupt evil manners."

Little Belle had not said much while the others were talking on this subject, but now she said quite softly to Bessie,—

"Bessie, do you think that I was a little sunbeam to Mabel? You know I said I wouldn't be; but papa told me that verse out of the Bible 'bout our Father making His sun to shine on the evil and the good, and he said that meant we ought to be good and like sunshine to everybody, if they were good or if they were bad."

"Yes: I do think you were, Belle," answered Bessie; "and I b'lieve our Father was very pleased with you, 'cause you know Mabel was pretty evil when she first came here; and it was very hard for you, most of all about the locket."

"Yes," said Belle, with a sigh; "and now I've had to make up my mind never to find my locket. Papa told me I had better. He says there is no hope of finding it now."

Meanwhile Maggie was congratulating Mabel still further on her improved conduct.

"We're very glad, Mabel," she said, "that we can be friends with you; for we wouldn't have liked you to be ' a heathen man and a publican' to us. We wouldn't like to be in that case with anybody, but 'specially with Belle's cousin, ' cause we're so very fond of her."

"So am I," said Mabel, looking affectionately over at Belle.

And this was true. Mabel had really learned to love Belle dearly and to trust her entirely; and, what was still better, she was becoming anxious to copy the pretty lady-like behavior, ready obedience, and sweet unselfishness, which she saw practised in the daily life of her cousin, and her little friends, Maggie and Bessie Bradford.

Not that it must be thought that all went smoothly on every occasion. Belle, as well as Mabel, had a firm will and a high temper, and she had been much indulged and somewhat spoiled by her father and nurse; so that now and then the two children would fall out about some trifle, and perhaps have some quick words, and, it might be, pout and sulk at one another for a while. But Belle was generally mindful of the " sunshine " she was to shed about her, and so was soon ready to make up and yield the disputed point; and then Mabel would be shamed into repentance, and there would be harmony and peace between them once more.

Yes: little Belle had truly proved a "sunbeam" to Mabel, throwing light upon the right way, and not only pointing it out to her so plainly that she could not miss it, but making it *look* so bright and attractive that she turned with some willingness to walk there, pleased to follow in the steps of her little example.

And the sunshine which she set herself to shed upon Mabel's way was reflected farther still on all about them, till where there had been discontent and weariness now reigned harmony and happiness; and all was peace.

Dora Johnson was a fat, chubby little thing, round as a ball, and like the "Dumpling" her school-mates called her; looking as if she was never troubled by a pain or an ache. But she was subject now and then to a pain and fulness in her head, for which the best remedy was a turn in the open air; and when one of these attacks came on in school, Miss Ashton always allowed her to go for this, knowing that Dora was a child to be trusted, who would return to her studies as soon as she was able. Taken in time, they passed away soon with but little trouble, and her kind teacher was watchful to prevent them as far as possible.

"Dora, my dear, does your head trouble you?" asked Miss Ashton, as she saw the child press her hand to her forehead, while her face flushed suddenly.

"Yes'm," answered Dora, dropping her book.

"Then wrap your cloak about you and go for a turn on the piazza or in the garden, till you are better," said the lady.

Dora gladly obeyed, thankful for the relief which the fresh, bracing air would bring to her throbbing head. Going for her cloak, she threw it around her, ran downstairs and out upon the piazza. Her step was light; and whatever sound her little feet might have made upon the floor was drowned by the loud and continuous hammering made by some workmen, who were tinning the roof of a neighboring house.

Dora walked once or twice the length of the piazza, and was beginning to feel better, when she heard the sound of voices below; and presently she saw the cook come out from the kitchen-door, followed by Marcia, the colored girl. Cook had a large bundle in her arm, and was evidently going out.

A door in the side of the garden-wall opened upon the street which bounded one side of it; and, unfastening this, the cook passed out, saying to Marcia,—

"Now mind and keep the door shut; and don't you be poking your head out, and leaving your work."

With which she disappeared; and Marcia shut and bolted the door, then cut one or two foolish antics as though she were pleased to be rid of her. She did not see Dora; for the end of the piazza where the little girl stood looking out at her was screened by a lattice over which ran a vine. There were no leaves on the vine now, it is true; but the stems and tendrils helped to make that corner a good hiding-place from any one who stood below.

Dora had no thought of hiding from Marcia; and she was about to speak to her, when she saw the colored girl, after looking carefully about her, stoop down, and with a bit of stick begin to poke and pry between the stones at the bottom of the wall, which was somewhat out of repair at this part, and showed one or two large cracks running along just above the ground.

"What can she be doing?" thought Dora; and curiosity held her silent till she should see what Marcia would be at.

Though hidden herself, she could see the girl very well, peeping down at her, as she did, through the lattice and the vine.

Marcia pried and pried, stopping now and then to look about her and listen, as if afraid of being caught; and at last fished up from between the stones something glittering which looked like — was it possible? — Dora thought it looked like a slender chain with something hanging to it. Could it be? — was it — Belle's locket?

She darted from her corner, along the piazza, down the steps leading to the garden, and around to the side of the wall where Marcia was; but the girl saw and heard her coming, and before she reached her the thing she had held in her hand was dropped again into its hiding-place between the stones.

Yet not so quickly but that Dora saw the motion of Marcia's hand, and she was more than ever convinced that something was wrong.

They stood and faced one another, the little lady and the colored girl: the former, stern and indignant, as became one who had caught a culprit in the act; the other, sheepish and guilty, wriggling her shoulders uneasily, and not daring to meet the eye which accused her.

"Give me that," said Dora, severely.

"Give you what, Miss Johnson?" said

Marcia, twisting and wriggling more than ever and vainly trying to put on an air of innocence.

"What you had in your hand. I b'lieve you've put it back in the wall, but you'll have to let me see it," said Dora.

"I ain't got nothin', Miss; and I s'pect Miss Ashton wants you. I hear her callin'," said Marcia.

"She's not calling, and if she was I wouldn't go till I knew what that was," answered Dora, firmly. "She'll excuse me when I tell her why."

Marcia persisted, and insisted that she had had nothing in her hand; but Dora knew better. And though the girl tried every device to rid herself of the young lady, she was not to be moved. She would mount guard over that hidden thing till she learned what it was, if she stood there all day.

Equally determined was Marcia; but she coaxed and threatened and tried to frighten in vain. Dora was a child of too much sense to be at all disturbed by the stories she told of what would happen to her; treated with scorn all the bribes which Marcia promised; and repeated over and over again her resolution not to stir till she saw what was in that crack.

As for Miss Ashton coming for her, it was just what Dora wished for: she could tell her teacher, and leave the matter in her hands, sure that she would find means of coming at the truth. And now there was Nelly Ransom's voice making itself heard.

"Dora! Dora! Where are you? Miss Ashton wants to know if you are worse."

"Come here, Nelly," said Dora; while Marcia grew more and more uneasy as she found the toils of her own wickedness closing down and down upon her. "You go and ask Miss Ashton to come here very quick. I've made a great discovery. Make haste."

Nelly obeyed, wondering much; and Miss Ashton, rather alarmed, speedily appeared on the spot.

Marcia, seeing that all was lost now, did not wait for her wickedness to be revealed; but, as the young lady came down the steps, shot away around the other side of the house and out of sight.

Dora's story was soon told, and the crack pointed out; in another moment the little girl and her teacher were busy following Marcia's example, and with bits of crooked stick trying to poke out the hidden "shiny thing," as Dora called it,— not yet sure enough to say the *locket*.

"Oh! Miss Ashton," said the excited child, "I feel something,— I do, I do!" and the next moment she drew up with her hooked stick — the locket! — yes, Belle's long-lost locket!

Dora's joy and exultation knew no bounds; and she would have rushed away with it to the school-room at once, had not Miss Ashton stopped her.

"Let me be the one to take it to Belle. Oh! do, Miss Ashton. I was the finder out," said the child.

"Yes, you shall give it to her; but I cannot have the class excited and disturbed just now," said the lady. "Besides, I want to know how this came here."

"But, Miss Ashton," said Dora, "I don't think I could keep it in. And then Mabel, poor Mabel! you wouldn't let any one think she stole it a minute longer, would you? Oh! I am so sorry I believed it of her, and was so ugly to her about it."

There was reason in Dora's words; and Miss Ashton, knowing that the curiosity of her young flock must already be excited, concluded to let her reveal her prize, although she felt sure that there would be little more study that morning if she did so.

It was singular how the locket should have come into Marcia's possession, and she did not yet feel that Mabel was quite cleared. But she gave Dora leave to make her good news known, and to restore the locket to Belle.

Away rushed Dora, and running into the school-room held aloft her prize, crying out,—

"Found! Found! and I did it, Belle and Mabel!"

Miss Ashton following close on Dora's steps found her class in quite as much commotion as she had expected. Belle, with the recovered locket held fast in her little hands, was covering it with kisses, while tears and smiles were struggling for the mastery. She flew into Miss Ashton's arms the moment she appeared, but could find no words for all that was in her heart.

But this could not be said for any of the others; for questions and exclamations were poured forth in such numbers that it was impossible to answer them all, and in spite of Miss Ashton's warning "Sh! sh!" there arose such a Babel of young voices that Mrs. Ashton opened the door of her room and asked the cause of the uproar.

A sudden hush fell upon the little ones when her voice was heard; and then Miss Ashton told in a few words where and how the locket had been found.

Belle waited till she was through, and then slipping from her teacher's lap ran over to Mabel, who sat sobbing at her desk; and the two little cousins put their arms about one another in a loving, congratulatory clasp.

"Oh! Mabel," said Belle, "I am so glad I b'lieved you didn't have it. I would feel so bad if I had."

"I'm so glad it's come out," sobbed Mabel, with a look and tone which went far towards convincing Miss Ashton that the child's story had really been true, and that, however mysterious it now seemed, Marcia in some way had obtained possession of the locket without Mabel's knowledge.

"So am I," said Dora, who had been one of the most forward in believing Mabel guilty; "and I'm so sorry I was hateful to you about it, Mabel. I'll make up to you for it as long as I live! See if I don't."

Congratulations were showered on both of the little cousins; and Belle's pleasure in the recovery of her locket was increased tenfold by knowing that Mabel was cleared.

For when, after some difficulty, Marcia was forced to confess how she had come by the locket, she said that on the day when she had been allowed to go to her sick sister, she had forgotten a bundle she was to take with her, and returned for it. Finding the gate unfastened, she came in without ringing, entered the house, and went up to her room without notice. But on the way up she saw Mabel run out from the school-room into the cloak-room, and peeping at her through the crack of the door saw her throw down some glittering object and cover it with her hat and sacque. She passed on her way; but, as she came down, was tempted to go in and see what the young lady had been hiding. At first it was only curiosity; but when she saw the pretty thing, the wish to have it came over her, and, the temptation proving too strong, she snatched it up, put the cloak and hat as she had found them, and ran away out of the house as quietly as possible, no one knowing that she had returned. But she dared not let any one see the locket, and she had put it for safe hiding in the crack in the wall, whence she could take it out once in a while and look at it. But it had been more trouble than pleasure to her; for Marcia had been taught better, and found truly that "the way of transgressors is hard."

She was not very penitent now, but very much frightened, believing that she would be sent to prison. This was not done of course; but Marcia's sin had deprived her of a good home and its comforts. Mrs. Ashton would have kept her, and still tried to do her good, if she had not had her young pupils to consider; but Marcia had been much given to pilfering of late; and this fault, so serious in any place, was particularly so in a school. So Marcia must go, in spite of all her promises, — promises made so often before, and so often broken. Mrs. and Miss Ashton still kept an eye upon her, and did what they could to befriend her; but she lost much through a sin which had brought her not the smallest pleasure.

And now we will say good-by for a while to Belle and Mabel; hoping that the latter, profiting by the lessons and example set before her, may also learn to draw light and brightness from the Sun of Righteousness, and herself prove a little sunbeam to all about her path.

530 Broadway, New York,
October, 1880.

Robert Carter & Brothers'
NEW BOOKS.

THE END OF A COIL. A Story. By the Author of the "Wide Wide World." 12mo. $1.75.

MY DESIRE. A Tale. By the Author of the "Wide Wide World." 12mo.

SUN, MOON, AND STARS. By Agnes Giberne. Illustrated. $1.50.

CHRIST AND HIS RELIGION. By Rev. John Reid. 12mo. $1.50.

RUE'S HELPS. By Jennie M. Drinkwater. $1.50.

TESSA WADSWORTH'S DISCIPLINE. By Jennie M. Drinkwater. 12mo. $1.50.

VOICES OF HOPE AND GLADNESS. By Ray Palmer, D.D. $1.50.

CARTERS' NEW BOOKS.

CHRISTIE'S OLD ORGAN, SAVED AT SEA, AND LITTLE FAITH. In one volume. $1.00.

WAS I RIGHT? A Story. By Mrs. WALTON, Author of "Christie's Old Organ." 5 illustrations. $1.00.

FLETCHER'S FAMILY DEVOTION. Royal quarto. 10 steel plates, cloth, gilt edges, $5.00.

SIX DAYS OF CREATION. By TAYLER LEWIS. 12mo. $1.50.

HESTER TRUEWORTHY'S ROYALTY. By the Author of "Win and Wear." $1.25.

MURIEL BERTRAM. A Tale. By AGNES GIBERNE. $1.50.

THE INTERPRETER'S HOUSE. SERMONS TO CHILDREN. By Rev. W W. NEWTON. $1.25.

New Books for Young People.

MARION SCATTERTHWAIT. A Tale of Work	$1.50
ELSIE GORDON. By Emily Brodie	1.25
EARL HUBERT'S DAUGHTER. By Miss Holt	1.50
NOBODY'S LAD	1.25
SOLDIERS OF THE CROSS	1.00
A ROSE WITHOUT THORNS. By Marshall	.50
THE VIOLET IN THE SHADE. "	.50
LIGHT ON THE LILY "	.50
DOLLY'S CHARGE "	.50
OUR LADDIE. By Miss Tomlinson	.50
URSULA. By Miss Bekenn	.50

*D'AUBIGNÉ'S HISTORY OF THE REFORMATION IN THE TIME OF CALVIN. Complete. 8 vols. 12mo. $8.00.

*D'AUBIGNÉ'S HISTORY OF THE REFORMATION IN THE SIXTEENTH CENTURY. 5 vols. $4.50.

www.ingramcontent.com/pod-product-compliance
Lightning Source LLC
Chambersburg PA
CBHW020803230426
43666CB00007B/824